At Issue

Is Racism a
Serious Problem?

Other Books in the At Issue Series:

At Issue

Is Racism a Serious Problem?

Aarti D. Stephens, Book Editor

GREENHAVEN PRESS
A part of Gale, Cengage Learning

GALE
CENGAGE Learning

Detroit • New York • San Francisco • New Haven, Conn • Waterville, Maine • London

Christine Nasso, *Publisher*
Elizabeth Des Chenes, *Managing Editor*

For more information, contact:
Greenhaven Press
27500 Drake Rd.
Farmington Hills, MI 48331-3535
Or you can visit our Internet site at gale.cengage.com

For product information and technology assistance, contact us at

Gale Customer Support, 1-800-877-4253
For permission to use material from this text or product, submit all requests online at www.cengage.com/permissions

Further permissions questions can be emailed to permissionrequest@cengage.com

Articles in Greenhaven Press anthologies are often edited for length to meet page requirements. In addition, original titles of these works are changed to clearly present the main thesis and to explicitly indicate the author's opinion. Every effort is made to ensure that Greenhaven Press accurately reflects the original intent of the authors. Every effort has been made to trace the owners of copyrighted material.

Cover photograph © Images.com/Corbis.

LIBRARY OF CONGRESS CATALOGING-IN-PUBLICATION DATA

Is racism a serious problem? / Aarti D. Stephens, book editor.
    p. cm. -- (At issue)
Includes bibliographical references and index.
ISBN 978-0-7377-4416-3 (hardcover)
ISBN 978-0-7377-4417-0 (pbk.)
1. Racism. 2. Racism--United States. I. Stephens, Aarti D.
HT1521.I718 2009
305.8--dc22
                                                        2008055436

Printed in the United States of America
1 2 3 4 5 6 7 13 12 11 10 09

Contents

Introduction

Americans elected Barack Obama as the 44th president of the United States on November 4, 2008. The first African American candidate to win the presidency, Obama's election was hailed as a "seismic event" in American history because of his racial background. The son of a black man of Kenyan descent and a white, American mother, Obama's candidacy highlighted the significance of race in America. While his election does not herald the end of racism in America, it marks a significant turning point in the history of race relations in the country. As columnist Joe Klein wrote in *Time* magazine, "Obama's victory creates the prospect of . . . a place where the primacy of racial identity . . . has been replaced by the celebration of pluralism, or cross-racial synergy."

Following the election, newspaper editorials enthusiastically hailed Obama's victory as having sounded the death knell for racism, with many observers pointing to Obama's popularity among Americans of all backgrounds as an indicator of real progress in race relations among blacks and whites. A headline in the *New York Times* on the day following Obama's election declared: "Racial Barrier Falls in Heavy Voter Turnout." While Obama has rarely defined himself as a black politician, he acknowledged the significance of being the first black American to win the presidency, and in his acceptance speech he noted his election was proof that "more than two centuries later, a government of the people, by the people and for the people has not perished from this Earth." Reporters on television noted that Obama's election attested that race and ethnicity were no longer important markers in mainstream American politics; voters from a variety of ethnic groups, cultures, and party affiliations turned out in record numbers to elect him, proving that the age of postracial politics had finally arrived in America. According to Nancy Gibbs, writing in a *Time* magazine article summarizing the election: "Barack Hussein Obama did not win because of the color of his skin. Nor did he win in spite of it."

Obama's victory, however, does not mean that racism and its accompanying problems have been eradicated from American political life. Even as Americans celebrated Obama's historic win, commentators acknowledged that race had been a significant factor in the election. For example, there were several instances during the 2008 primaries and general election when the issue of race became a major topic of discussion. The most noteworthy among these occurred in early 2008, following the release of videotapes containing incendiary, race-based remarks made by Obama's then-pastor, Reverend Jeremiah Wright. Obama's campaign quickly responded by clarifying its candidate's positions versus those expressed by Wright. In one of the most powerful speeches of his political career, Obama spoke about the issue of race in America, acknowledging its sensitive place in American life. In his attempt to answer the charges of reverse-racism and anti-Americanism leveled at him based on Wright's remarks, Obama stressed that although his own candidacy was inextricably linked to his race and background, his nomination was ultimately successful because of a message that transcended racial divisions. Ultimately, Obama noted, the controversy over Wright's comments is reflective of "the complexities of race in this country that we've never really worked through—a part of our union that we have yet to perfect."

The focus on Obama's background through the entire election cycle, and the strong feelings generated by the Wright controversy, highlighted the continuing significance of race in the minds of many Americans. Obama himself has written about the importance of race in America—and has expanded the debate to include other minorities. While acknowledging the singularity of his achievement as a black man, he stressed in his book, *The Audacity of Hope*, that his own multi-racial background does not allow him the luxury of "restricting [his] loyalties on the basis of race." Instead, he wrote, the discussion about race in America must expand beyond conflict between black and white to include the concerns of other minority groups in America, including Latinos and Asians. Obama and many other contemporary black leaders, including such personalities as Tennessee politician Harold Ford, Jr., and Newark, New Jersey mayor Cory Booker, view themselves as representatives of a new generation of minority politicians. A 2001 report by the Joint Center for Political and Economic Studies pointed out significant "generational differences" among black elected officials from the 1970s–1980s compared to those who have gained prominence in recent decades. This new group of politicians presents a sharp contrast to many older black political leaders, including Jesse Jackson and Al Sharpton, who rose to prominence after the Civil Rights era—as such, their status was based on, and indeed they used, their backgrounds as black Americans to gain support among the black community. The new generation of black and minority politicians characterized most prominently by Obama, is more focused on such issues as eradicating poverty and improving schools than they are in proving their "authenticity" as true representatives of their own ethnic groups, be they black, Latino, or Asian. As a result, they enjoy a wider level of support among Americans of all backgrounds.

This shift in perspective is very real and highlights the progress made by race relations. At the same time, it also reveals gaps in the road to true racial and ethnic equality as Americans struggles to integrate people from a wide variety of backgrounds. In an increasingly global economy, America are being forced to contend with shifting economic and cultural realities that are far more complex than the old divisions between black and white. The increase in immigrant populations, especially from Latin America, and the rise of globalization have driven many traditionally racial wedge-issues of the

1970s and 1980s, such as crime, welfare, and affirmative action, to the periphery. Instead, theorized Peter Beinart in *Time*, "as the face of America has changed, so has American racism." Beinart contended that. Americans are now more likely to associate dark skin with foreignness, and school segregation complaints now more often refer to the drain on resources caused by immigrant children forcing schools to spend millions of dollars on English-language classes, rather than issues of racial integration. Since the terrorist attacks of September 11, 2001, fears and anxieties about cultural bias and strains caused by economic shifts in American industry have fused together and frequently manifest themselves in fear and anxiety regarding foreigners in general.

So while fifty years ago, America's racial challenges arose from within, our current challenges stem from a fear of outsiders as we struggle to come to terms with new economic realities forced on us by emerging and developing economies in countries such as India and China. In this context, many commentators view Obama, with his global, multicultural background, as the personification of the new face of race and culture in America. Thus, predicted Michael C. Moynihan, in the political journal *Reason*, Obama's election to the presidency will be a landmark achievement in two ways—first, it will help soothe long-standing resentments among many black Americans who regard his election as the final frontier to true equality. And second, it will force Americans to put the black/white conflict to rest, allowing us to begin assimilating new cultural and ethnic realities that denote the next chapter of race relations in the country.

Addressing a crowd of thousands in Chicago during his victory speech in 2008, Obama acknowledged the power and symbolism of his election, noting that it was a moment when Americans "put their hand on the arc of history," bending it in a new direction. The sentiment was echoed in newspaper editorials across the nation the following morning, with Thomas Friedman declaring in the *New York Times* that "We awake this morning to a different country ... the Civil War is over. Let reconstruction begin." Similarly, Michael Gerson wrote in the *Washington Post* that "An African American will take the oath of office blocks from where slaves were once housed .... Every event, every act will complete a cycle of history.... The most dramatic possible demonstration that the promise of America—so long deferred—is not a lie." Thus, as one era closes in the history of American race relations, another one begins. Summarizing the importance of the 2008 presidential election, Texas pastor T.D. Jakes noted that while Obama's victory did not erase all racial tensions, it did point the way for "black, white, and brown [to] melt into a brilliant depiction of red, white, and blue."

1

Prejudice Is a Natural Tendency That May Be Overcome

Mark Buchanan

Mark Buchanan is an American-born author and physicist based in Europe.

Humans tend to judge each other based on ethnic, racial, and religious markers. Although ethnic prejudice has resulted in negative implications for minorities in modern times, bias toward one's own group is a natural human tendency that has helped us survive by fostering increased cooperation and commonality among people of the same ethnicity. Our awareness of the anthropology behind ethnic groupings may help us find ways to consciously curb unacceptable racist tendencies.

In 1992, during the war between Serbia and Croatia, the *Washington Post* ran an interview with a Croatian farmer named Adem, who had a horrific story to tell. Over the previous year, Adem said, discourse between local Serbs and Croats had deteriorated, as individual identities dissolved into a menacing fog of "us" versus "them". Then group animosity turned into something far worse. Serbs from a neighbouring village abruptly rounded up 35 men from Adem's village and slit their throats. The summer before, the killers had helped their victims harvest their crops.

[In 2007] a small group of Z-list celebrities caused an international incident during the filming of the UK version of

Mark Buchanan, "Born Prejudiced," *New Scientist*, vol. 193, March 17–23, 2007, pp. 40–44. Copyright © 2007 Reed Elsevier Business Publishing, Ltd. Reproduced by permission.

the reality TV show *Big Brother*. The seemingly racist comments made by Jade Goody and her cronies to Bollywood film star Shilpa Shetty provoked thousands of shocked viewers to write letters of complaint. There was a media frenzy. Questions were asked in Parliament. Even the [then] Chancellor of the Exchequer, Gordon Brown, who happened to be on a visit to India, felt he had to comment on the affair.

Ethnic Markers as Guides

Two very different stories; one common theme. Proof, if it were needed, that the human tendency to judge others in the crudest terms—race, religion, ethnicity, or any arbitrary marker—has not been consigned to the history books, no matter how much we might wish it were so. Somewhat disturbingly, scientists now suggest that this is not really surprising because such prejudice is part of human nature.

If they are correct, then the roots of group animosity and hatred run very deep indeed, which may be depressing news for those trying to make a difference in ethnic or sectarian hotspots from Darfur and Iraq to inner cities and football terraces. Yet researchers also insist that facing up to our authentic nature is the only way to gain real insight into the forces that drive group conflict, and to learn how we might manage and defuse such urges. "We shouldn't treat prejudice as pathological just because it offends us," says anthropologist Francisco Gil-White. "If we aim to transcend ethnic strife, we would be wise to understand the role that perfectly normal human psychology plays in producing it."

Psychologists have long known of our proclivity to form "in groups" based on crude markers, ranging from skin colour to clothing styles. Think of inner-city gangs, Italian football supporters, or any "cool" group of stylish teenagers. "Our minds seem to be organised in a way that makes breaking the human world into distinct groups almost automatic," says psychologist Lawrence Hirschleld of the University of Michigan,

Ann Arbor. Many experiments confirm this, and show that we tend to favour our own group, even when that group is just an arbitrary collection of individuals.

Race and ethnicity are arbitrary markers that have acquired meaning.

In 1970, for example, a team of researchers led by psychologist Henri Tajfel of the University of Bristol, UK, randomly divided teenage boys from the same school into two groups, and gave every boy the chance to allocate points to two other boys, one from each group. This could be done in different ways—some increasing the combined total for both recipients, and others increasing the difference between the two. The boys consistently chose options of the latter kind, favouring recipients from their own group. Experiments like these are enough to convince Tajfel and others that if you put people into different groups, call them red and blue, north and south, or whatever, a bias towards one's own group will automatically emerge.

This in itself does not make us racist. In fact it may not be such a bad thing: research published last year [2006] suggests at least one useful function of our groupist tendencies. Political scientists Ross Hammond of the Brookings Institution in Washington, DC, and Robert Axelrod of the University of Michigan have discovered, perhaps surprisingly, that it can promote cooperation. Taking their cue from Tajfel's finding that in-group favouritism emerges with minimal prompting, Hammond and Axelrod decided to try to emulate this in a simple computer model. Imagine a population of individuals, interacting in pairs at random, and engaging in some activity where both would benefit from cooperation, but each was also tempted to cheat—getting more for themselves at the other's expense. With no insight into the likely behaviour of others, individuals in such a world would have no way—besides pure guesswork—to maximise the outcome of their interactions. But add one simple element, colour, and everything changes.

People in Hammond and Axelrod's world come in four colours, assigned randomly at birth. When interacting with others, they might now adopt one of several basic strategies. An individual might act randomly, as before, ignoring colour—which would make sense as the colours say nothing about how an individual is likely to behave. Alternatively, a person might always cooperate or always cheat, regardless of the other's colour. Another option would be to follow a groupist "ethnocentric" strategy—cooperating with anyone of the same colour, but always trying to cheat those of another colour. Finally, agents might be anti-groupist—only cooperating with someone of another colour. The researchers randomly assigned one of these strategies to each agent. They also gave all agents the ability to learn from one another, so that any strategy that did well would tend to be copied and so spread.

Groups Help Us Survive

What happened then, they discovered, was that agents of each particular colour began to gather together. At first, a few groupist agents of the same colour might find themselves together by chance. Within such a group, cooperative interactions lead to good outcomes, causing others nearby to copy their strategy, swelling the group. In the model, Hammond and Axelrod found that strongly ethnocentric groups of different colours came to fill the world, at the expense of others. Anyone who did not follow the groupist strategy tended to suffer. Even someone ignoring colour—and remember colour initially signified nothing about an agent's behaviour—would also get wiped out. In short, once people begin to act on colour, it comes to matter. What's more, it turns out that the overall level of cooperation is higher in this world where there is group favouritism than in a world where agents are colourless. "Ethnocentrism is actually a mechanism for generating cooperation, and one that does not demand much in the way of cognitive ability," says Hammond.

Axelrod and Hammond are well aware that their model is a far cry from the complexities of real-world racism. Still, it is interesting that colour prejudice emerges even though colour has no intrinsic significance. Modern genetics has dispelled the naive notion that racial divisions reflect real biological differences. We know that the genetic variation between individuals within one racial or ethnic group is generally much larger than the average difference between such groups. As in the virtual world, race and ethnicity are arbitrary markers that have acquired meaning. But you won't get far telling Blacks and Hispanics in the racially charged areas of Los Angeles that their differences are just "superficial" cultural constructs. "Race doesn't matter because it is real," says historian Niall Ferguson of Harvard University, "but because people conceive it to be real."

What's more, this misconception seems to be deeply ingrained in our psyche. For example, Hirschfeld found that by the age of 3 most children already attribute significance to skin colour. In 1993, he showed a group of children a drawing of a chubby black child dressed up as a policeman, followed by photos of several adults, each of whom had two of the three traits: being black, chubby and dressed as a policeman. Asked to decide which person was the boy as a grown-up, most children chose a black adult even though he was either not overweight or minus a police uniform. "Kids appear to believe," says Hirschleld, "that race is more important than other physical differences in determining what sort of person one is."

More recent brain imaging studies suggest that even adults who claim not to be racist register skin colour automatically and unconsciously. In 2000, a team led by social psychologist Allan Hart of Amherst College in Massachusetts found that when white and black subjects viewed faces of the other race both showed increased activity in the amygdala—a brain region involved in grasping the emotional significance of stimuli. Yet consciously, these subjects reported feeling no emotional difference on seeing the different faces. In another study of white subjects, in the same year, neuroscientist Elizabeth Phelps of New York University and colleagues found that those individuals whose amygdala lit up most strongly also scored highest on a standard test for racial prejudice.

A far better way to decide who can be trusted and who cannot is to assess an individual's character and personality rather than to rely on meaningless markers.

Does this mean that our species has evolved to see the world in terms of black and white? Not necessarily. After all, our ancestors would not normally have met people whose skin was a different colour from their own: neighbouring ethnic groups would have looked pretty much alike. So, it's possible that our tendency to classify people by colour might simply be a modern vice, learned early and reinforced throughout our lives—even, paradoxically, by anti-racist messages. That seems unlikely, however, when you consider our attitudes toward ethnicity. In field work among Torguud Mongols and Kazakhs, neighbouring ethic groups living in central Asia, Gil-White investigated ideas of ethnic identity to find out whether people link it more with nurture (a child being brought up within a group) or nature (the ethnicity of biological parents). The majority of both groups saw ethnicity as a hidden but powerful biological factor, unaffected by someone being adopted into another group. "They perceive the underlying nature as some kind of substance that lies inside and causes the members of an ethnic group to behave the way they do," he says. Like race, ethnicity has no biological significance, yet this is exactly how we perceive it.

Ethnic Differences Are a Modern Problem

Many researchers now believe that we have evolved a tendency to divide the world along ethnic lines. For example, anthropologist Rob Boyd from the University of California, Los Angeles, argues that our ancestors, given the rich social context of human life, would have needed skills for perceiving the important groups to which individuals belonged. Being attuned to ethnic differences would have allowed individuals to identify others who shared the same social norms—people with whom it would have been easiest to interact because of shared expectations. It would have paid to attend to cultural differences such as styles of clothing, scarification or manner of greeting that marked one group out from another. In the modern world, colour is simply mistaken as one such marker.

That might explain why we tend to divide the world into groups and why we use ethnic differences and skin colour as markers to help us do this. It even gives a rationale for in-group favouritism. But what about out-group animosity? Is prejudice part of the whole evolved package? Gil-White believes it is. He argues that within any group of people sharing social norms, anyone who violates those will attract moral opprobrium—it is considered "bad" to flout the rules and benefit at the expense of the group. This response is then easily transferred to people from other ethnic groups. "We're tempted to treat others, who are conforming to their local norms, as violating our own local norms, and we take offence accordingly," says Gil-White.

As a result we may be unconsciously inclined to see people from other ethnic groups not simply as different, but as cheats, morally corrupt, bad people.

Natural but Not Nice

"I think all this work refutes those naive enough to believe that if it weren't for bad socialising, we would all be nice tolerant people who accept cultural and ethnic differences easily," says Daniel Chirot, professor of international studies at the University of Washington, Seattle. That may sound disturbing, but being biologically primed for racism does not make it inevitable. For a start, what is natural and biological needn't be considered moral or legal.

"The sexual attraction that a grown man feels for a 15-year-old female is perfectly natural," Gil-White points out. But most societies forbid such relations, and all but a very few men can control their urges.

Besides, if ethnocentrism is an evolved adaptation to facilitate smooth social interactions, it is a rather crude one.

A far better way to decide who can be trusted and who cannot is to assess an individual's character and personality rather than to rely on meaningless markers. In today's world, that is what most of us do, most of the time. It is only when it becomes difficult to judge individuals that people may instinctively revert to the more primitive mechanism. Hammond and Axelrod argue that this is most likely to happen under harsh social or economic conditions, which may explain why ethnic divisions seem to be exaggerated when societies break down, as a consequence of war, for example. "To me this makes perfect sense," says Chirot. "Especially in times of crisis we tend to fall back on those with whom we are most familiar, who are most like us."

Knowing all this, it may be possible to find ways to curb our unacceptable tendencies. Indeed, experiments show how little it can take to begin breaking down prejudice. Psychologist Susan Fiske from Princeton University and colleagues got students to view photos of individuals from a range of social groups, while using functional MRI to monitor activity in their medial prefrontal cortex (mPFC), a brain region known to light up in response to socially significant stimuli. The researchers were shocked to discover that photos of people belonging to "extreme" out-groups, such as drug addicts, stimulated no activity in this region at all, suggesting that the viewers considered them to be less than human. "It is just what you see with homeless people or beggars in the street," says Fiske, "people treat them like piles of garbage." In new experiments, however, she was able to reverse this response. After replicating the earlier results, the researchers asked simple, personal questions about the people in the pictures, such as, "What kind of vegetable do you think this beggar would like?" Just one such question was enough to significantly raise activity in the mPFC. "The question has the effect of making the person back into a person," says Fiske, "and the prejudiced response is much weaker."

It would appear then that we have a strong tendency to see others as individuals, which can begin to erode our groupist instincts with very little prompting. Perhaps this is why, as Chirot points out, ethnocentrism does not always lead to violence. It might also explain why in every case of mass ethnic violence it has taken massive propaganda on the part of specific political figures or parties to stir passions to levels where violence breaks out.

If the seeds of racism are in our nature, so too are the seeds of tolerance and empathy. By better understanding what sorts of situations and environments are conducive to both, we may be able to promote our better nature.

2

The Perception of Racism Has Eclipsed Actual Racism

Shelby Steele

Shelby Steele is a research fellow at the Hoover Institution, and he specializes in the study of race relations, multiculturalism, and affirmative action. In 2006 he received the Bradley Prize for his contributions to the study of race in America. Steele has written several books on the subject of race relations, including White Guilt: How Blacks and Whites Together Destroyed the Promise of the Civil Rights Era.

Race continues to be a powerful force in society—84 percent of blacks and 66 percent of whites view it as a serious problem in American life. White supremacy, once a legitimate force that maintained white dominion over world resources and societies, is now a truly unacceptable notion. The nature of racism has changed, so although it continues to exist, racism now is different from the historical, systematic oppression of black people. It has assumed a different kind of power, making it impossible for blacks or whites to acknowledge that issues such as poverty, broken families, and lack of education are far more significant problems for blacks than racism. Although white oppression was the initial cause of many of these issues, the solution to the economic underdevelopment of black communities lies within those communities, and will be solved only when the idea of racism as an article of faith is rejected.

Shelby Steele, "Does Racism Matter?" *Hoover Digest*, Winter 2007, pp. 76–79. Copyright © 2007 by the Board of Trustees of the Leland Stanford Junior University. Reproduced by permission.

From a police shooting in Queens, N.Y., to a racially charged legal battle involving the Los Angeles Fire Department, from the self-immolation of comedian Michael Richards to the failed Senate campaign of Tennessee's Harold Ford, race is back in the news, bringing with it a batch of new and disturbing questions.

Is racism now a powerful, subterranean force in our society? Is it so subtly infused into the white American subconscious as to be both involuntary and invisible to the racist himself? A recent CNN poll tells us that 84 percent of blacks and 66 percent of whites think racism is a "very serious" or "somewhat serious" problem in American life. Is this true?

White Supremacy Defeated

In attempting to answer these questions, we must acknowledge one of the most profound achievements in recent human history: the death of white supremacy. Here was an event far more world-altering than the collapse of communism, and yet, out of a truly extraordinary historical blindness, it has gone utterly unnoticed. Possibly it was an event too conspicuous to see.

Many believe that it is racist for whites to say white supremacy is dead and that it is Uncle Tomism for blacks to say it. But it is dead nevertheless. Once a legitimate authority with dominion over all the resources and peoples of the world, it is today universally seen as one of history's greatest evils. It is dead today because it has no authority anywhere in the world and no legitimacy out of which to impose itself. It was defeated by revolutions in the last half of the twentieth century that spanned the globe from India to Algeria to the United States. It was defeated by the people who had suffered it. And even if it survives in some quarters as an idea, as a speculation, it now stigmatizes anyone associated with it to the point of ruin.

When Richards blasted forth with the "N-word" at a comedy club, his language met with universal condemnation. Today's acts of racism play out within an American society obsessed with purging itself of racism, a society that measures its very legitimacy by its intolerance for racism. When I was growing up in the last decade of segregation, even violent acts of racism were no threat to American legitimacy. When Richards said to his hecklers, "Fifty years ago we would have hung you up by your feet," he was longing for the days of my childhood, when blacks would fear to heckle a white comic—a time when violence enforced a much larger pattern of black subjugation. But Richards' hecklers only laughed at him. The difference between the two eras is the death of white supremacy.

The incentive to make racism into a faith ... has destroyed our ability to know the reality of racism in America.

This does not mean that racist behavior today is somehow benign. It means that today racism swims upstream in an atmosphere of ferocious intolerance. Moreover, today's racism is no longer in concert with an overt and systematic subjugation of blacks. Although racism continues to exist, it no longer stunts the lives of blacks.

Victimization Mentality

Yet a belief in the ongoing power of racism is, today, an article of faith for "good" whites and "truth-telling" blacks. It is heresy for any white or black to say openly that, today, underdevelopment and broken families are vastly greater problems for blacks than racism, even though this is obviously true. The problem is that this truth blames the victim. It suggests that black progress will come more from black effort than from white goodwill—even though white oppression caused the underdevelopment in the first place.

In other words, this truth is unfair. And when whites or blacks utter it, they are instantly identified with the unfairness rather than with the truth. So propriety causes us to say that racism still explains black difficulty.

This explanation is also a source of power because it portrays blacks as victims. And wherever there are victims, there is justification for seeking power in their name. Thus the specter of black difficulty has been an enormous source of power for the left since the 1960s. To say racism is not the first cause of black problems is to put yourself at odds with the post-'60s Left's most enduring fount of power.

This of course means that racism in the United States has parallel lives. In one life, it is the actual instances of racism on the ground. But, in its parallel life, it is a time-honored currency of power that still trades well in the United States. Here, racism lives as faith rather than fact. It is something you believe in out of unacknowledged self-interest.

So when race gets in the news, it is hard to know whether we are dealing with fact or faith. Was the political ad that some say defeated Harold Ford in Tennessee really racist, as the NAACP suspects, or was this old civil rights group ambulance-chasing for power? Did racism motivate the police shooting in Queens? Was the recent defeat of affirmative action at the polls in Michigan an example of racism or of an insistence on fairness? As we look at such events, are we judging facts or practicing a faith?

The great mistake Americans made after the civil rights victories of the '60s was to allow race to become a government-approved means to power. Here was the incentive to make racism into a faith. And its subsequent life as a faith has destroyed our ability to know the reality of racism in America. Today we live in a terrible ignorance that will no doubt last until we take race out of every aspect of public life—until we learn, as we did with religion, to separate it from the state.

3

Diversity Cannot Be Mandated to Communities

James Q. Wilson

James Q. Wilson is Ronald Reagan professor of public policy at Pepperdine University in California, and the author of several books, including Moral Judgment, American Government *and* Thinking About Crime.

Ethnic and racial diversity is an important social characteristic in neighborhoods because, in the long run, it promotes connections between different social groups, reducing ethnocentric behavior. According to political scientist Robert D. Putnam, ethnically integrated neighborhoods help solidify social solidarity by helping create new, inclusive social identities. In the short term, however, it is difficult for people to adapt to ethnically diverse surroundings. Studies focusing on the impact of diversity on the social well-being of neighborhoods prove that ethnically diverse neighborhoods currently rate consistently below ethnically homogenous neighborhoods. Mixed ethnic groups reveal a lower level of social trust across different groups, resulting in little or no group unity. Forced integration, such as initiatives helping minorities gain access to communities where they have never lived before, are limited in their ability to promote true ethnic integration. Although the legal system should be used to strike down blatantly racist policies, government mandates forcing diversity into neighborhoods will not be successful until families

James Q. Wilson, "Bowling with Others," *Commentary*, vol. 124, October 2007, pp. 30–33. Copyright © 2007 by the American Jewish Committee. All rights reserved. Reproduced by permission of the publisher and the author.

find common ground on their own, based on similar moral values. These values cross ethnic lines, and can form a strong basis for true integration.

In his celebrated book *Bowling Alone*, the political scientist Robert D. Putnam argued that America, and perhaps the Western world as a whole, has become increasingly disconnected from family, friends, and neighbors. We once bowled in leagues; now we bowl alone. We once flocked to local chapters of the PTA [Parent Teacher Association], the NAACP [National Association for the Advancement of Colored People], or the Veterans of Foreign Wars; now we stay home and watch television. As a result, we have lost our "social capital"—by which Putnam meant both the associations themselves and the trustworthiness and reciprocity they encourage. For if tools (physical capital) and training (human capital) make the modern world possible, social capital is what helps people find jobs and enables neighborhoods and other small groupings of society to solve problems, control crime, and foster a sense of community.

Social Capital and Communities

In *Bowling Alone*, Putnam devised a scale for assessing the condition of organizational life in different American states. He looked to such measures as the density of civic groups, the frequency with which people participate in them, and the degree to which (according to opinion surveys) people trust one another. Controlling for race, income, education, and the like, he demonstrated that the higher a state's level of social capital, the more educated and affluent are its children, the lower the murder rate, the greater the degree of public health, and the smaller the likelihood of tax evasion. Nor is that all. High levels of social capital, Putnam showed, are associated with such civic virtues as greater tolerance toward women and minorities and stronger support for civil liberties. But all of these good things have been seriously jeopardized by the phenomenon he identified as "bowling alone."

After finishing his book, Putnam was approached by various community foundations to measure the levels of social capital within their own cities. To that end he conducted a very large survey: roughly 30,000 Americans, living in 41 different communities ranging downward in size from Los Angeles to Yakima, Washington, and even including rural areas of South Dakota. He published the results this year [2007] in a long essay in the academic journal *Scandinavian Political Studies* on the occasion of his having won Sweden's prestigious Johan Skytte prize.

Putnam's new essay takes an in-depth look not at social capital per se but at how "diversity"—meaning, for this purpose, racial and ethnic differences—affects our lives in society. Such diversity is increasing in this country and many others, if for no other reason than immigration, and so Putnam has tried to find out how it changes the way people feel about their neighbors, the degree of their confidence in local government, their willingness to become engaged in community-wide projects, and their general happiness.

When ethnic groups are mixed there is weaker social trust, less car pooling, and less group cohesion.

The ethnic and racial diversity that Putnam examines is widely assumed to be very good for us. The more time we spend with people different from us, it is said, the more we will like and trust them. Indeed, diversity is supposed to be so good for us that it has become akin to a national mandate in employment and, especially, in admissions to colleges and universities. When the Supreme Court decided the [*University of California v.*] *Bakke* case in 1978, the leading opinion, signed by Justice Lewis Powell, held that although a university was not allowed to use a strict numerical standard to guarantee the admission of a fixed number of minority students, it could certainly "take race into account," on the theory that a racially diverse student body was desirable both for the school and for society at large.

As a result of this and similar court rulings, not only colleges but many other institutions began invoking the term "diversity" as a justification for programs that gave preferences to certain favored minorities (especially blacks and Hispanics). Opponents of these programs on constitutional and civil-liberties grounds were put in the difficult position of appearing to oppose a demonstrated social good. Did not everyone know that our differences make us stronger?

But do they? That is where Putnam's new essay comes in. In the long run, Putnam argues, ethnic and racial diversity in neighborhoods is indeed "an important social asset," because it encourages people to form connections that can reduce unproductive forms of ethnocentrism and increase economic growth. In his words, "successful immigrant societies create new forms of social solidarity and dampen the negative effects of diversity by constructing new, more encompassing identities."

Whatever his beliefs about the positive effects of diversity in the long run, however—not only does he consider it a potentially "important social asset," but he has written that it also confers "many advantages that have little or nothing to do with social capital"—Putnam is a scrupulous and serious scholar (as well as a friend and former colleague at Harvard [University]). In the *short* run, he is frank to acknowledge, his data show not positive effects but rather the opposite. "The more ethnically diverse the people we live around," he writes, "the less we trust them."

Diversity, Putnam concludes on the basis of his findings, makes us "hunker down." Not only do we trust our neighbors less, we have less confidence in local government, a lowered sense of our own political efficacy, fewer close friends, and a smaller likelihood of contributing to charities, cooperating with others, working on a community project, registering to vote—or being happy.

Diversity and improved solidarity have gone hand in hand only in those institutions characterized by enforced authority and discipline.

Of course many of these traits can reflect just the characteristics of the people Putnam happened to interview, rather than some underlying condition. Aware of the possibility, Putnam spent a great deal of time "kicking the tires" of his study by controlling statistically for age, ethnicity, education, income or lack of same, poverty, homeownership, citizenship, and many other possible influences. But the results did not change. No matter how many individual factors were analyzed, every measure of social well-being suffered in ethnically diverse neighborhoods—and improved in ethnically homogeneous ones.

Diversity and Neighborhoods

"Shocking" is the word that one political scientist, Scott Page of the University of Michigan, invoked to describe the extent of the negative social effects revealed by Putnam's data. Whether Putnam was shocked by the results I cannot say. But they should not have been surprising; others have reported the same thing. The scholars Anil Rupasingha, Stephan J. Goetz, and David Frewater, for example, found that social capital across American counties, as measured by the number of voluntary associations for every 10,000 people, goes up with the degree of ethnic homogeneity. Conversely, as others have discovered, when ethnic groups are mixed there is weaker social trust, less car pooling, and less group cohesion. And this has held true for some time: people in Putnam's survey who were born in the 1920's display the same attitudes as those born in the 1970's.

Still, Putnam believes that in the long run ethnic heterogeneity will indeed "create new forms of social solidarity." He offers three reasons. First, the American military, once highly segregated, is today anything but that—and yet, in the Army and the Marines, social solidarity has increased right alongside greater ethnic diversity. Second, churches that were once highly segregated, especially large evangelical ones, have likewise become entirely and peaceably integrated. Third, people who once married only their ethnic kin today marry across ethnic and religious (and, to a lesser degree, racial) lines.

I can offer a fourth example: organized sports. Once, baseball and football teams were made up of only white or only black players; today they, too, are fully integrated. When Jackie Robinson joined the Brooklyn Dodgers in 1947, several teammates objected to playing with him, and many fans heckled him whenever he took the field. Within a few years, however, he and the Dodgers had won a raft of baseball titles, and he was one of the most popular figures in the country. Today such racial and ethnic heckling has virtually disappeared.

Unfortunately, however, the pertinence of the military, religious, or athletic model to life in neighborhoods is very slight. In those three institutions, authority and discipline can break down native hostilities or force them underground. Military leaders proclaim that bigotry will not be tolerated, and they mean it; preachers invoke the word of God to drive home the lesson that prejudice is a sin; sports teams (as with the old Brooklyn Dodgers) point out that anyone who does not want to play with a black or a Jew is free to seek employment elsewhere.

But what authority or discipline can anyone bring to neighborhoods? They are places where people choose to live, out of either opportunity or necessity. Walk the heterogeneous streets of Chicago or Los Angeles and you will learn about organized gangs and other social risks. Nor are these confined to poor areas: Venice, a small neighborhood in Los Angeles where several movie stars live and many homes sell for well over $1 million, is also a place where, in the Oakwood area, the Shoreline Crips and the V-13 gangs operate.

In many a neighborhood, ethnic differences are often seen as threats. If blacks or Hispanics, for whatever reason, are more likely to join gangs or commit crimes, then whites living in a neighborhood with many blacks or Hispanics will tend to feel uneasy. (There are, of course, exceptions: some, especially among the well-educated, prefer diversity even with all its risks.) Even where everyone is equally poor or equally threatened by crime, people exhibit less trust if their neighborhood is ethnically diverse than if it is homogeneous.

Of Putnam's three or four reasons for thinking that ethnic heterogeneity will contribute to social capital in the long run, only one is compelling: people are indeed voluntarily marrying across ethnic lines. But the paradoxical effect of this trend is not to preserve but to blunt ethnic identity, to the point where it may well reduce the perception of how diverse a neighborhood actually is. In any case, the fact remains that diversity and improved solidarity have gone hand in hand only in those institutions characterized by enforced authority and discipline.

Strong families living in neighborhoods made up of families with shared characteristics seem much more likely to bring their members into . . . associational life.

The legal scholar Peter H. Schuck has written an important book on this issue. In *Diversity in America*, he examines three major efforts by judges and government officials to require racial and income diversity in neighborhoods. One of them banned income-discrimination in the sale and rental of housing in New Jersey towns. Another enabled blacks who were eligible for public housing to move into private rental units in the Chicago suburbs. In the third, a federal judge attempted to diversify residential patterns in the city of Yonkers, New York, by ordering the construction of public housing in middle-class neighborhoods selected by him.

Although the Chicago project may have helped minorities to enter communities where they had never lived, the New Jersey and Yonkers initiatives had little effect. As Schuck writes, "Neighborhoods are complex, fragile, organic societies whose dynamics outsiders cannot readily understand, much less control." A court can and should strike down racist public policies, but when it goes beyond this and tries to mandate "diversity," it will sooner or later discover that it "cannot conscript the housing market to do its bidding."

People who celebrate diversity . . . are endorsing only one part of what it means to be a complete human being, neglecting morality.

Reducing Segregation

Taking a different approach, Thomas Schelling, a Nobel laureate in economics, has shown in a stimulating essay that neighborhood homogeneity and even segregation may result from small, defensible human choices that cannot themselves be called racist. In fact, such choices can lead to segregation even when the people making them expressly intend the opposite. Suppose, Schelling writes, that blacks and whites alike wish to live in a neighborhood that is (for example) half-white and half-black. If one white family should come to think that other white families prefer a community that is three-fourths white, and may move out for that reason, the first white family is itself likely to move out in search of its own half-white, half-black preference. There is no way to prevent this.

Schelling's analysis casts a shadow of doubt on Putnam's own policy suggestions for reducing the disadvantages and stimulating the benefits of ethnic heterogeneity. Those suggestions are: investing more heavily in playgrounds, schools, and athletic fields that different groups can enjoy together; extending national aid to local communities; encouraging churches to reach out to new immigrants; and expanding public support for the teaching of English.

The first recommendation is based on the implicit assumption that Schelling is wrong and on the even more dubious assumption that playgrounds, schools, and athletic fields—things Putnam did not measure in his survey—will increase the benefits of diversity even when age, income, and education do not. The second is empty: Putnam does not say what kind of aid will produce the desired effects. If he is thinking of more housing, Schuck has already shown that providing this usually does not increase diversity. If he is thinking of education, in the 1970's federal judges imposed forced busing in an effort to integrate schools; it was an intensely unpopular strategy, both among those whose children were being bused and among those whose neighborhoods were being bused into.

The third proposal, encouraging outreach by churches, might well make a difference, but how do we go about it? Require people to attend an evangelical church? Would Robert Putnam attend? I suspect not. And as for the final recommendation, teaching English at public expense to everyone, it is a very good idea—provided one could break the longstanding attachment of the education establishment to bilingual instruction.

Shared Values Increase Unity

Whether we should actually seek to transform the situation described by Putnam's data is another question. I do not doubt that both diversity and social capital are important, or that many aspects of the latter have declined, though perhaps not so much as Putnam suspects. But as his findings indicate, there is no reason to suppose that the route to the latter runs through the former. In fact, strong families living in neighborhoods made up of families with shared characteristics seem much more likely to bring their members into the associational life Putnam favors. Much as we might value both heterogeneity and social capital, assuming that the one will or should encourage the other may be a form of wishful thinking.

That is because morality and rights arise from different sources. As I tried to show in *The Moral Sense*, morality arises from sympathy among like-minded persons: first the family, then friends and colleagues. Rights, on the other hand, grow from convictions about how we ought to manage relations with people not like us, convictions that are nourished by education, religion, and experience.

People who celebrate diversity (and its parallel, multiculturalism) are endorsing only one part of what it means to be a complete human being, neglecting morality (and its parallel, group and national pride). Just as we cannot be whole persons if we deny the fundamental rights of others, so we cannot be whole persons if we live in ways that discourage decency, cooperation, and charity.

In every society, people must arrange for trade-offs between desirable but mutually inconsistent goals. James Madison [fourth president of the United States], in his famous *Federalist* Number Ten, pointed to just this sort of trade-off when he made the case for a large national government that would ensure the preservation of those individual rights and liberties that are at risk in small communities. When it comes to the competing values of diversity and the formation of social capital, as when it comes to other arrangements in a democracy, balance is all.

4

Environmental Harm Disproportionately Impacts the Poor and Minorities

Leyla Kokmen

Leyla Kokmen is the program coordinator for the Health Journalism graduate program at the University of Minnesota. She also has worked as a staff reporter for several newspapers, including the Seattle Times *and the* Denver Post.

Poor and minority neighborhoods show clear evidence of environmental disparity, including increased pollution, unsanitary living conditions, and little or no regulated control of the environmental conditions. The environmental justice movement, along with other activists and social scientists, began working on resolving this issue with the launch of several protests against the location of landfills and other hazardous waste in poor neighborhoods. Over the years, this movement has increased its scope to include holistic solutions that encourage poor people and minorities to participate actively in the environmental movement as it pertains to their neighborhoods. Focusing on issues of public health and community development, modern activists should address environmental problems as part of a larger solution that brings new jobs and opportunities to poor and minority neighborhoods.

Manuel Pastor ran bus tours of Los Angeles a few years back. These weren't the typical sojourns to Disneyland or the MGM studios, though; they were expeditions to some of the city's most environmentally blighted neighborhoods— where railways, truck traffic, and refineries converge, and where people live 200 feet from the freeway.

The goal of the "toxic tours," explains Pastor, a professor of geography and of American studies and ethnicity at the University of Southern California (USC), was to let public officials, policy makers, and donors talk to residents in low-income neighborhoods about the environmental hazards they lived with every day and to literally see, smell, and feel the effects.

"It's a pretty effective forum," says Pastor, who directs USC's Program for Environmental and Regional Equity, noting that a lot of the "tourists" were eager to get back on the bus in a hurry. "When you're in these neighborhoods, your lungs hurt."

How do we get the work, wealth, and health benefits of the green economy to the people who most need those benefits?

Modern Environmental Activists

Like the tours, Pastor's research into the economic and social issues facing low-income urban communities highlights the environmental disparities that endure in California and across the United States. As stories about global warming, sustainable energy, and climate change make headlines, the fact that some neighborhoods, particularly low-income and minority communities, are disproportionately toxic and poorly regulated has, until recently, been all but ignored.

A new breed of activists and social scientists are starting to capitalize on the moment. In principle they have much in common with the environmental justice movement, which came of age in the late 1970s and early 1980s, when grassroots groups across the country began protesting the presence of landfills and other environmentally hazardous facilities in predominantly poor and minority neighborhoods.

In practice, though, the new leadership is taking a broader-based, more inclusive approach. Instead of fighting a proposed refinery here or an expanded freeway there, all along trying to establish that systematic racism is at work in corporate America, today's environmental justice movement is focusing on proactive responses to the social ills and economic roadblocks that if removed would clear the way to a greener planet.

The new movement assumes that society as a whole benefits by guaranteeing safe jobs, both blue-collar and white-collar, that pay a living wage. That universal health care would both decrease disease and increase awareness about the quality of everyone's air and water. That better public education and easier access to job training, especially in industries that are emerging to address the global energy crisis, could reduce crime, boost self-esteem, and lead to a homegrown economic boon.

That green rights, green justice, and green equality should be the environmental movement's new watchwords.

"This is the new civil rights of the 21st century," proclaims environmental justice activist Majora Carter.

A lifelong resident of Hunts Point in the South Bronx, Carter is executive director of Sustainable South Bronx, an eight-year-old nonprofit created to advance the environmental and economic future of the community. Under the stewardship of Carter, who received a prestigious MacArthur Fellowship in 2005, the organization has managed a number of projects, including a successful grassroots campaign to stop a planned solid waste facility in Hunts Point that would have processed 40 percent of New York City's garbage.

Her neighborhood endures exhaust from some 60,000 truck trips every week and has four power plants and more than a dozen waste facilities. "It's like a cloud," Carter says. "You deal with that, you're making a dent."

The first hurdle Carter and a dozen staff members had to face was making the environment relevant to poor people and people of color who have long felt disenfranchised from mainstream environmentalism, which tends to focus on important but distinctly nonurban issues, such as preserving Arctic wildlife or Brazilian rainforest. For those who are struggling to make ends meet, who have to cobble together adequate health care, education, and job prospects, who feel unsafe on their own streets, these grand ideas seem removed from reality.

Expanding the Green Movement

That's why the green rights argument is so powerful: It spans public health, community development, and economic growth to make sure that the green revolution isn't just for those who can afford a Prius. It means cleaning up blighted communities like the South Bronx to prevent potential health problems and to provide amenities like parks to play in, clean trails to walk on, and fresh air to breathe. It also means building green industries into the local mix, to provide healthy jobs for residents in desperate need of a livable wage.

Historically, mainstream environmental organizations have been made up mostly of white staffers and have focused more on the ephemeral concept of the environment rather than on the people who are affected. . . . Today, though, as climate change and gas prices dominate public discourse, the concepts driving the new environmental justice movement are starting to catch on. Just recently, for instance, *New York Times* columnist Thomas Friedman dubbed the promise of public investment in the green economy the "Green New Deal."

Van Jones, whom Friedman celebrated in print last October, is president of the Ella Baker Center for Human Rights in

Oakland, California. To help put things in context, Jones briefly sketches the history of environmentalism:

The first wave was conservation, led first by Native Americans who respected and protected the land, then later by Teddy Roosevelt, John Muir, and other Caucasians who sought to preserve green space.

The second wave was regulation, which came in the 1970s and 1980s with the establishment of the Environmental Protection Agency (EPA) and Earth Day. Increased regulation brought a backlash against poor people and people of color, Jones says. White, affluent communities sought to prevent environmental hazards from entering their neighborhoods. This "not-in-my-backyard" [NIMBY] attitude spurred a new crop of largely grassroots environmental justice advocates who charged businesses with unfairly targeting low-income and minority communities. "The big challenge was NIMBY-ism," Jones says, noting that more toxins from power plants and landfills were dumped on people of color.

The third wave of environmentalism, Jones says, is happening today. It's a focus on investing in solutions that lead to "eco-equity." And, he notes, it invokes a central question: "How do we get the work, wealth, and health benefits of the green economy to the people who most need those benefits?"

Poor Communities Suffer Most

There are a number of reasons why so many environmental hazards end up in the poorest communities.

Property values in neighborhoods with environmental hazards tend to be lower, and that's where poor people—and often poor people of color—can afford to buy or rent a home. Additionally, businesses and municipalities often choose to build power plants in or expand freeways through low-income neighborhoods because the land is cheaper and poor residents have less power and are unlikely to have the time or organizational infrastructure to evaluate or fight development.

"Wealthy neighborhoods are able to resist, and low-income communities of color will find their neighborhoods plowed down and [find themselves] living next to a freeway that spews pollutants next to their schools," USC's Manuel Pastor says.

Moreover, regulatory systems, including the EPA and various local and state zoning and environmental regulatory bodies, allow piecemeal development of toxic facilities. Each new chemical facility goes through an individual permit process, which doesn't always take into account the overall picture in the community. The regulatory system isn't equipped to address potentially dangerous cumulative effects.

In a single neighborhood, Pastor says, you might have toxins that come from five different plants that are regulated by five different authorities. Each plant might not be considered dangerous on its own, but if you throw together all the emissions from those static sources and then add in emissions from moving sources, like diesel-powered trucks, "you've created a toxic soup," he says.

In one study of air quality in the nine-county San Francisco Bay Area, Pastor found that race, even more than income, determined who lived in more toxic communities. That 2007 report, "Still Toxic After All These Years: Air Quality and Environmental Justice in the San Francisco Bay Area," published by the Center for Justice, Tolerance & Community at the University of California at Santa Cruz, explored data from the EPA's Toxic Release Inventory, which reports toxic air emissions from large industrial facilities. The researchers examined race, income, and the likelihood of living near such a facility.

More than 40 percent of African American households earning less than $10,000 a year lived within a mile of a toxic facility, compared to 30 percent of Latino households and fewer than 20 percent of white households.

As income rose, the percentages dropped across the board but were still higher among minorities. Just over 20 percent of

African American and Latino households making more than $100,000 a year lived within a mile of a toxic facility, compared to just 10 percent of white households.

The same report finds a connection between race and the risk of cancer or respiratory hazards, which are both associated with environmental air toxics, including emissions both from large industrial facilities and from mobile sources. The researchers looked at data from the National Air Toxics Assessment, which includes estimates of such ambient air toxics as diesel particulate matter, benzene, and lead and mercury compounds. The areas with the highest risk for cancer had the highest proportion of African American and Asian residents, the lowest rate of home ownership, and the highest proportion of people in poverty. The same trends existed for areas with the highest risk for respiratory hazards.

According to the report, "There is a general pattern of environmental inequity in the Bay Area: Densely populated communities of color characterized by relatively low wealth and income and a larger share of immigrants disproportionately bear the hazard and risk burden for the region."

Framing the environmental debate in terms of opportunities will engage the people who need the most help.

The Impact of Racism

Twenty years ago, environmental and social justice activists probably would have presented the disparities outlined in the 2007 report as evidence of corporations deliberately targeting minority communities with hazardous waste. That's what happened in 1987, when the United Church of Christ released findings from a study that showed toxic waste facilities were more likely to be located near minority communities. At the 1991 People of Color Environmental Leadership Summit, leaders called the disproportionate burden both racist and genocidal.

In their 2007 book *Break Through: From the Death of Environmentalism to the Politics of Possibility*, authors Ted Nordhaus and Michael Shellenberger take issue with this strategy.... They argue that some of the research conducted in the name of environmental justice was too narrowly focused and that activists have spent too much time looking for conspiracies of environmental racism and not enough time looking at the multifaceted problems facing poor people and people of color.

"Poor Americans of all races, and poor Americans of color in particular, disproportionately suffer from social ills of every kind," they write. "But toxic waste and air pollution are far from being the most serious threats to their health and well-being. Moreover, the old narratives of intentional discrimination fail to explain or address these disparities. Disproportionate environmental health outcomes can no more be reduced to intentional discrimination than can disproportionate economic and educational outcomes. They are due to a larger and more complex set of historic, economic, and social causes."

Today's environmental justice advocates would no doubt take issue with the finer points of Nordhaus and Shellenberger's criticism—in particular, that institutional racism is a red herring. Activists and researchers are acutely aware that they are facing a multifaceted spectrum of issues, from air pollution to a dire lack of access to regular health care. It's because of that complexity, however, that they are now more geared toward proactively addressing an array of social and political concerns.

"The environmental justice movement grew out of putting out fires in the community and stopping bad things from happening, like a landfill," says Martha Dina Argüello, executive director of Physicians for Social Responsibility–Los Angeles, an organization that connects environmental groups with doctors to promote public health. "The more this work gets done, the more you realize you have to go upstream. We need to stop bad things from happening."

"We can fight pollution and poverty at the same time and with the same solutions and methods," says the Ella Baker Center's Van Jones.

Poor people and people of color have borne all the burden of the polluting industries of today, he says, while getting almost none of the benefit from the shift to the green economy. Jones stresses that he is not an environmental justice activist, but a "social-uplift environmentalist." Instead of concentrating on the presence of pollution and toxins in low-income communities, Jones prefers to focus on building investment in clean, green, healthy industries that can help those communities. Instead of focusing on the burdens, he focuses on empowerment.

Spreading the Message

With that end in mind, the Ella Baker Center's Green-Collar Jobs Campaign plans to launch the Oakland Green Jobs Corps this spring. The initiative, according to program manager Aaron Lehmer, received $250,000 from the city of Oakland and will give people ages 18 to 35 with barriers to employment (contact with the criminal justice system, long-term unemployment) opportunities and paid internships for training in new energy skills like installing solar panels and making buildings more energy efficient.

The concept has gained national attention. It's the cornerstone of the Green Jobs Act of 2007, which authorizes $125 million annually for "green-collar" job training that could prepare 30,000 people a year for jobs in key trades, such as installing solar panels, weatherizing buildings, and maintaining wind farms. The act was signed into law in December as part of the Energy Independence and Security Act.

While Jones takes the conversation to a national level, Majora Carter is focusing on empowerment in one community at a time. Her successes at Sustainable South Bronx include the creation of a 10-week program that offers South Bronx and other New York City residents hands-on training in brownfield remediation and ecological restoration. The organization has also raised $30 million for a bicycle and pedestrian greenway along the South Bronx waterfront that will provide both open space and economic development opportunities.

As a result of those achievements, Carter gets calls from organizations across the country. In December [2007] she traveled to Kansas City, Missouri, to speak to residents, environmentalists, businesses, and students. She mentions exciting work being done by Chicago's Blacks in Green collective, which aims to mobilize the African American community around environmental issues. Naomi Davis, the collective's founder, told Chicago Public Radio in November [2007] that the group plans to develop environmental and economic opportunities—a "green village" with greenways, light re-manufacturing, ecotourism, and energy-efficient affordable housing—in one of Chicago's most blighted areas.

Carter stresses that framing the environmental debate in terms of opportunities will engage the people who need the most help. It's about investing in the green economy, creating jobs, and building spaces that aren't environmentally challenged. It won't be easy, she says. But it's essential to dream big.

"It's about sacrifice," she says, "for something better and bigger than you could have possibly imagined."

5

Racism Is a Significant Problem in the Penal System

Stuart Taylor, Jr.

Stuart Taylor, Jr. is a nonresident senior fellow at the Brookings Institution, a nonprofit public-policy organization focused on independent research on politics and government. Taylor is also a contributing editor for Newsweek *magazine as well as a columnist for the* National Journal.

Although examples of unwarranted prosecutions among minority defendants still abound, there has been a decline in discriminatory practices within the judicial system in general. However, the penal system continues to foster racial injustice due to mandatory sentencing laws regarding the possession of crack cocaine that inadvertently target black Americans. By focusing heavily on drug offenses and other crimes most likely to be committed by blacks, coupled with severe sentencing laws, the system may force nonviolent drug offenders toward violence as a result of incarceration that may be out of balance with the nature of the original crime.

It is regrettable that the legend of the "Jena Six" has for many become the leading symbol of the grave injustices to African-Americans that pervade our nation's penal system. The legend is partly false. And the notion that racism is the main reason for the injustices to hundreds of thousands of black defendants around the nation is entirely false.

To be sure, there is still too much racism among prosecutors, judges, and jurors. But this is far less widespread and virulent, even in Jena, La., than Al Sharpton and Jesse Jackson—the media-anointed (albeit, repeatedly discredited) African-American "leaders"—like to pretend. There are still too many unwarranted prosecutions of innocent minority (and other) defendants, as detailed in my August 4 [2007] column, "Innocents in Prison." But the vast majority of those prosecuted are guilty, as may prove to be the case with some or all of the Jena Six.

Rather, the heart of the racial injustice in our penal system is the grossly excessive punishment of hundreds of thousands of nonviolent, disproportionately black offenders whose long prison terms ruin countless lives and turn many who could have become productive citizens into career criminals.

Sentencing Laws to Blame

The Supreme Court heard two cases on October 2 [2007] that focus on a relatively small piece of this problem: how much discretion federal district judges have to depart from federal sentencing guidelines that provide savagely severe prison terms for small-time drug offenders, among others. The most savage penalties of all are for people—overwhelmingly, black people—caught with fairly small amounts of crack cocaine.

But the justices, hemmed in by wrong-headed mandatory sentencing laws, are merely rearranging deck chairs on the Titanic, no matter how they rule. Nothing that the Court will ever do could make much of a dent in the overly punitive regime that has sent the number of prisoners in this country soaring to 2.2 million, more than in any other nation. This represents more than a *sixfold* increase in the number of incarcerated Americans since 1970, when it was 330,000. More than 40 percent of these prisoners are black. And according to a recent study by the nonprofit Sentencing Project, 500,000 of the 2.2 million are locked up for drug crimes, and a majority of the convicted drug prisoners have no history of violence or high-level drug-selling.

Such are the fruits of decades of tough-on-crime posturing by politicians. Now a bipartisan group in Congress is pushing to alleviate some of the most excessive penalties, especially in crack cases. This is a small blessing. But the proposed tinkering is a far cry from the enormous policy changes needed. A more hopeful sign was a Joint Economic Committee hearing set by Sen. Jim Webb, D-Va., for October 4 [2007] titled "Mass Incarceration in the United States: At What Cost?"

But in the end, only a vast change of attitude on the part of the voters, and in turn among the state and federal officials they elect, could return sanity to the system.

With our bloated incarceration rates, especially for nonviolent drug crimes, "the system takes men with limited education and job skills and stigmatizes them in a way that makes it hard for them to find jobs, slashes their wages when they do find them, and brands them as bad future spouses," as Christopher Shea wrote in a September 23 [2007] column in the *Boston Globe*. "The effects of imprisonment ripple out from prisoners, breaking up families and further impoverishing neighborhoods, creating the conditions for more crime down the road."

Our penal system visits these dire consequences on a staggeringly high percentage of the African-American population. More than 22 percent of all black men in their early 30s and more than half of the subset who dropped out of high school have spent time behind bars. These percentages are far higher than they were during the worst era of American apartheid.

Is this situation the fault of white racism? Well, the main reason that an overly punitive system has such a severe effect on black men is that they commit hugely disproportionate numbers of crimes. As *The Economist* points out, "Young black men are seven times more likely to be jailed than whites, but they are also seven times more likely to murder someone, and their victims are usually black."

Disproportionate Penalties

The absurdly excessive penalties for possessing or selling crack cocaine could be seen as evidence that many white voters and legislators are subconsciously more willing to throw away the lives of small-time black offenders than small-time white offenders. You can call that racism, but only by stretching the word. Especially since the most severe crack cocaine sentences of all had strong support in the Congressional Black Caucus when they were adopted in 1986 and thereafter. Black officials hoped that long prison terms would quiet the "crack wars" that were then consuming inner cities. The Clinton administration also supported these laws.

Focusing mainly on the residue of racism is a distraction from the far bigger problem of over-punishment.

Orlando Patterson, the noted African-American sociology professor at Harvard, put his finger on the main source of racial injustice in a September 30 [2007] *New York Times* op-ed:

"This virtual gulag of racial incarceration [reflects] a law enforcement system that unfairly focuses on drug offenses and other crimes more likely to be committed by blacks, combined with draconian mandatory sentencing and an absurdly counterproductive retreat from rehabilitation [of] offenders. [This system] simply makes hardened criminals of nonviolent drug offenders and spits out angry men who are unemployable, unreformable, and unmarriageable."

In short, focusing mainly on the residue of racism is a distraction from the far bigger problem of over-punishment. It is also a distraction from understanding why African-American crime rates are so high.

The reason, Patterson says, is "something that has been swept under the rug for too long in black America: the crisis in relations between men and women of all classes and, as a result, the catastrophic state of black family life, especially among the poor. . . . The resulting absence of fathers—some 70 percent of black babies are born to single mothers—is undoubtedly a major cause of youth delinquency."

The Jena Six

This is not to deny that the Jena case involved a clear injustice to identifiable African-Americans. Nor is it necessarily to deny the (debatable, in my view) assertions that Jena school authorities and/or the local district attorney used a racial double standard favoring white students over blacks.

The clear injustice was the initial use of a grossly excessive charge—attempted second-degree murder—that could have doomed five of the Jena Six to long prison terms for ganging up on Justin Barker, a white student who was neither attacked with a deadly weapon nor seriously injured. Indeed, after a much-needed outcry the charges were reduced to aggravated second-degree battery.

The 10,000 to 20,000 African-Americans who traveled to Jena from all over the country on September 20 [2007] also protested that the authorities allowed white students who hung nooses on a tree and got into fights to escape serious punishment, while throwing the book at the blacks who attacked Justin Barker.

But even if that's true, the Jena case is far from being the civil-rights morality play scripted by Sharpton, Jackson, and some in the media. Contrary to their spin, the December 4, 2006, gang attack on Barker was no "schoolyard fight." Nor was it a direct response to the deplorable (but noncriminal) hanging of nooses on a schoolyard tree by *other* white students *more than three months earlier.*

In fact, then-16-year-old Mychal Bell, who had been arrested four times for alleged violent offenses, is accused of knocking Barker unconscious in an unprovoked, blindside attack. Then, the charges say, all of the Jena Six (or seven, as it now appears) stomped the prostrate victim until an uninvolved student intervened. Barker was briefly hospitalized with a concussion and multiple bruises.

The Real Reasons Why So Many African Americans Are in Prison

"In American law," as James Kirchick wrote in the gay online magazine *Advocate.com,* "you are not entitled to beat a defenseless and innocent person because someone with the same skin color as that person offended you months earlier."

Imagine for a moment that the races of the Jena students had been reversed, and that six whites had ganged up on a lone black student. I suspect that there might have been an even bigger Sharpton-Jackson-led protest. But instead of attacking the prosecutor for being too hard on the black thugs who beat up a solitary victim, the protesters would have been demanding that the white thugs be imprisoned for "hate crimes." And so would some of the same media commentators who have decried the prosecutions of the Jena Six.

They would do better to turn their fire on the real reasons why so many African-Americans end up in prison: cruel sentencing laws, crummy education, and weak families.

6

African Americans Are Disadvantaged Due to Poverty and Inequality

Michael B. Katz and Mark J. Stern

Michael B. Katz and Mark J. Stern teach at the University of Pennsylvania; Katz is a professor of history, while Stern is a professor of social welfare and history as well as codirector of the Urban Studies Program. They have coauthored One Nation Divisible: What America Was and What It Is Becoming.

Reports by the Pew Research Center and Brookings Institution issued in November 2007, highlighted the fragile nature of African American success in the United States. Although African Americans have made huge strides toward equal rights, black inequality is, increasingly, a product of the growing income gap between black and white families rather than previously established forms of public and private discrimination. Many African Americans acknowledge a widening gap between the values held in high regard by middle-class black Americans versus those from poorer backgrounds. This dichotomy has resulted in divisions within the black community; in contrast, social values have converged across racial groups, and are increasingly common across different racial groups based on economic status rather than ethnic background. Despite the progress in place, more needs to be done to ensure that poverty among African Americans does not displace overt racism as a barrier to ultimate equality.

Michael B. Katz and Mark J. Stern, "Beyond Discrimination: Understanding African American Inequality in the Twenty-First Century," *Dissent*, vol. 55, Winter 2007, pp. 61–65. Copyright © 2007 by Foundation for the Study of Independent Social Ideas, Inc. Reproduced by permission.

In November 2007, two reports by distinguished research centers turned African American inequality into national news. Their startling and discomfiting data highlighted both the fragility of African American success and the widening fault lines that divide African Americans from each other. Impressive and authoritative as the reports are, they nonetheless remain incomplete because they do not explain how and why African American inequality has changed during the last several decades or the place of gender and publicly supported work in the new black equality. These omissions matter because adequate and realistic responses to the issues raised by the reports require grasping the sources of the revolutionary changes that have left blacks at once more and less equal. Black inequality no longer results from powerful and interlocking forms of public and private discrimination and oppression. Rather, it is the product of processes beginning with childhood that sort African Americans into more or less favored statuses, differentiating them by class and gender. This new African American inequality, and the poverty that accompanies it requires policies that identify key points of intervention and reassert a vigorous role for government in the promotion of economic security and upward mobility. In this article, we summarize our research findings about the new African American inequality and comment on its implications. Readers interested in a more fully documented version should consult either our article "The New African American Inequality" in the *Journal of American History* or book, *One Nation Divisible: What America Was and What It Is Becoming.*

The Face of Inequality

The November 2007 reports by the Pew Research Center and Brookings Institution describe, respectively, growing values gaps among African Americans and the failure of their increased incomes to match white incomes or assure economic security to their children. The Pew report concluded that "African Americans see a widening gulf between the values of middle class and poor blacks, and nearly four-in-ten say that because of the diversity within their community, blacks can no longer be thought of as a single race." Black respondents also were less optimistic about black progress than at any time since 1983; lacked confidence in the fairness of the criminal justice system; and believed that "anti-black discrimination is commonplace in everyday life," views that set them apart from whites. Both blacks and whites, however, agree that in the last decade "values held by blacks and whites" have converged. The good news is that "black and white Americans express very little overt racial animosity." About eight in ten hold "a favorable view about members of the other group"; most think that blacks and whites get along at least "pretty well"; and "more than eight-in-ten adults in each group also say they know a person of a different race whom they consider a friend."

The Brookings report focuses on economic mobility. It shows that income gaps between blacks and whites persist, despite increases among both groups. This income growth masks declining incomes for both black and white men in their thirties whose family incomes rose only because women's incomes increased, with white women's income growth outpacing black women's. In 2004, the median black family income for people ages thirty to thirty-nine was 58 percent of white family income, or $35,000 compared to $60,000. At first glance, the statistics of intergenerational mobility appear more promising: 63 percent of black children earn more than their parents, with incomes adjusted for inflation. But "a majority of blacks born to middle-income parents grow up to have less income than their parents. Only 31 percent of black children born to parents in the middle of the income distribution have family income greater than their parents" compared to 68 percent of white children from similar backgrounds. Similarly, a majority—54 percent—of black children born to the poorest parents remain, themselves, at the bottom of the economic ladder. For the poorest white children the proportion—31 percent—is much lower.

Both the Pew and Brookings reports underscore the persistence of group inequality and the differentiation of African American social structure. This pattern reflects what we call the paradox of inequality. Despite repeated contractions and expansions in the degree of economic inequality, throughout modern American history the income and wealth pyramid has remained durable and steep, with continuities in the distribution of rewards by work, ethnicity, and gender. Yet, immense individual and group mobility has accompanied this structural durability. To make the process concrete, consider this: in the last half of the twentieth century, the civil rights movement and the women's movement swept across the United States. Although neither reached all its goals, each gained many of its objectives and, in the process, transformed the nation and the life experience of tens of thousands of women and men. Yet, in the decades of the movements' greatest successes, Americans became massively more unequal, with, for example, between 1973 and 2004, the real annual income of the poorest 20 percent of Americans rising 20 percent while that of the wealthiest fifth soared 73 percent. This coexistence of structural rigidity with individual and group fluidity is what we mean by the paradox of inequality.

The History of Inequality

Inequality, however, has not always worked in the same way. At the start of the twentieth century pervasive, overt racial discrimination barred blacks from most jobs, denied them equal education, and disenfranchised them politically. After mid-century, slowly and sometimes with violent opposition, the situation of African Americans changed dramatically. Courts and Congress—prodded by a massive social movement, national embarrassment on the world stage during the Cold War, and the electoral concerns of urban politicians—

extended political and civil rights. Affirmative action and new "welfare rights" contributed to the extension of social citizenship—guarantees of food, shelter, medical care, and education. By the end of the century, legal and formal barriers that had excluded blacks from most institutions and from the most favorable labor market positions largely had disappeared. Black poverty had plummeted, and black political and economic achievements were undeniable.

Yet, for many people—both white and black—the sense remained that racism still pervaded American society, operating in both old and new ways, removing some barriers but erecting others. Observers found discrimination in racial profiling by police; verbal slips by members of Congress; disproportionate poverty, incarceration, and capital punishment; and in the workings of institutions and public policies that disadvantaged blacks. Racism, they maintained, kept African Americans residentially segregated and clustered disproportionately in the least desirable jobs, if not out of the work force altogether, and circumscribed their opportunities for education, high incomes, and the accumulation of wealth. Far more often than whites, African Americans lived in poverty. Most black children were born out-of-wedlock, and a very large fraction of them grew up poor. And in the 1980s and 1990s, some indices of black economic progress began to reverse direction. In the summer of 2005, television images of New Orleans' African Americans, segregated in low-lying sections of the city, many without automobiles, trapped as floodwaters rose [following Hurricane Katrina], brought home in a horrible way the persistence and consequences of black inequality and poverty.

Was the glass half empty or half full? Could past black achievement be projected into the future or had it stalled, leaving this enduring categorical inequality rooted deeply into the soil of American life? This is the question implicit in the Pew and Brookings reports. The question should not be framed in either/or terms or answered using a single scale of progress, for the historic pattern of black in equality based on social, economic, and political exclusion was in fact largely shattered in the course of the century, to be rearranged in a new configuration of inequality. In the early twentieth century, the sources and results of America's black/white divide overlapped with and reinforced one another. What stands out about the new pattern of inequality is the *cumulative* process from which it results and the internal differentiation that is its product. Inequality among African Americans no longer grows out of a massive and mutually reinforcing, legal and extralegal, public and private system of racial oppression. Rather, it is a subtler matter, proceeding through a series of screens that filter African Americans into more or less promising statuses, progressively dividing them along lines full of implications for their economic futures and, in the face of natural disaster, their very lives. The history of African American experience reflects the paradox of inequality in twentieth-century America.

Blacks less often acquired a four-year college education; men (but not women) who did enter remunerative jobs earned less than whites. With education held constant, in fact, black women had reached income parity with white women. Nonetheless, whatever their jobs or educations, African Americans could not bundle individual into family earnings as large as those of whites; more of them were poor; more men were in prison; they owned homes less frequently; and the homes they did own were not worth as much. As a consequence, they lived in segregated neighborhoods, owned automobiles less often, died younger, and, when disaster hit, proved the most vulnerable. Economic inequality, thus, was a *cumulative* process.

Blacks in the American Workforce

The recomposition of the patterns of inequality occurred between the end of the Second World War and the turn of the century. Although blacks did not reach economic equality with whites, the configurations of inequality among them had been transformed irrevocably. A differentiation within African American social structure—a differentiation by labor-force participation, industrial employment, occupation, education, income, wealth, and gender—was one result. While both black men and women moved into white-collar work, women's gains outpaced men's. Between 1940 and 2000, 63 percent of black women—an increase from only 7 percent in 1940—compared to 52 percent of black men, worked at white-collar jobs. Clearly, the expansion of government, education, health care, and private-sector white-collar jobs opened a plethora of opportunities seized by African American women. For black women, America's economic transition from manufacturing to service was a source of opportunities gained, not lost. At the same time, the situation of black men worsened as disturbing numbers found themselves outside the labor market altogether. For instance, between 1940 and 2000, the proportion of black men in the twenty-one to twenty-five age group who were out of the labor force jumped from 9 percent to 34 percent.

It was through this process of differentiation—the accumulation of many small and not-so-small distinctions—that black social structure divided and that black inequality endured despite individual and group mobility. This is the structural reality that underlies the Pew report's discovery of the "widening gulf between the values of middle class and poor blacks."

Even when African Americans, both women and men, moved into better types of occupations, they clustered in less prestigious and well-paid positions. Among professional and technical workers, for example, black women were employed more often than white women as technicians, the lowest rung on the ladder. Black professional men worked twice as often as white men in the human services, the least well-paying branch of the professions. Group mobility could not overcome the nation's most historically durable inequality.

Everywhere, in one way or another, the hand of government, for better or worse, is evident in the inequality story—from sanctioned racial segregation, for instance, to legislation supportive of trade unions and fair wages to civil rights. But the example on which we want to focus briefly here is less well known: the facilitation of African American social mobility.

Many black men found employment in public and state-related jobs (that is, jobs that were nominally private but dependent on public funding). In 2000, these state-related industries employed 19 percent of black men. Public and state-related employment proved even more important for black women: at century's end nearly half (43 percent) of African American women worked in state-related industries.

Black poverty and inequality ... are problems of national imagination and will.

Public Employment

Public employment became African Americans' distinctive occupational niche. The *Brown v. Board of Education* Supreme Court decision (1954), which declared school segregation unconstitutional, the Civil Rights Act (1964), the Voting Rights Act (1965), and affirmative action policies in the 1960s and 1970s: all built pressure to desegregate work and expand opportunities for African Americans. Racial barriers to employment crumbled most quickly and widely in state-related jobs when their numbers exploded in the 1960s and 1970s as the War on Poverty and the Great Society escalated spending on social programs. These were good jobs. They paid, on the whole, more than private-sector employment. In 2000, the median income of African Americans who worked full time in the public sector exceeded the income of black private-sector employees by 15 percent for men and 19 percent for women. Public and state-related employment, thus, have proved the most powerful vehicles for African American economic mobility and the most effective antipoverty legacy of the Great Society. This dependence on publicly funded work also left African Americans vulnerable. Reductions in public employment and spending strike them with special ferocity and undermine their often fragile achievements.

Public employment, more than blue-collar factory jobs, played a key role in lifting African Americans out of poverty. High black poverty rates, that is, did not result from deindustrialization. Aside from Detroit and Chicago, African Americans did not find extensive work in major cities in manufacturing and were denied the best industrial jobs. Even where black industrial work was common, service jobs remained the core of black urban employment. Black industrial workers, moreover, did not earn higher wages or work more steadily than African Americans employed in other sorts of work. In a sample of fifteen representative cities in 1949, Buffalo, New York, had the largest fraction of black industrial workers, except for Detroit, but its black poverty rate was among the highest. In cities with the lowest black poverty rates, relatively few African Americans worked in industrial jobs. Instead, government employment, which accounted for 60 percent of the variance in black poverty rates across the fifteen cities, reduced poverty and proved the best predictor of African American poverty rates. Public employment did more than reduce poverty by providing steady, well-paid jobs. African American access to public employment also signaled increasing black political influence, which, in turn, encouraged local welfare bureaucracies to respond more generously to black need. Thus, in cities with the highest levels of public employment more blacks escaped poverty through public transfer programs—the size of black public employment explained 33 percent of the effectiveness of cities' public assistance programs. Overall, the correlation between African Americans' poverty rate and employment in government was a striking-0.7.

What We Can Do

What, then is the moral of this history of black poverty and inequality whose consequences the Pew and Brookings reports highlight so vividly? In his commentary on the reports, African American scholar Henry Louis Gates, Jr., rightly observes that the "historical basis for the gap between the black middle and underclass shows that ending discrimination, by itself, would not eradicate black poverty and dysfunction." But neither is his remedy, by itself, adequate to the task. "Perhaps a bold and innovative approach to the problem of black poverty," he writes, "would be to turn tenants into homeowners ... for the black poor, real progress may come only once they have an ownership stake in American society." For support, Gates points to the huge disparities in black and white wealth. Economist Edward N. Wolff found the median net worth of non-Hispanic black households in 2004 to be $11,800 compared to $118,300 for whites, with most of the difference accounted for by real estate.

Taking a leaf from Margaret Thatcher's book, as Gates suggests, by turning residents of public housing into homeowners would not solve the problem. Despite the privatization of public housing, poverty remains high in Britain. There, social housing, as it is more often called in Europe, is not restricted to the very poor as it is in the United States. Its tenants include many of the employed working class with incomes sufficient to pay mortgages and maintenance costs. In the United States, moreover, a stunning rise in homeownership has not wiped out black poverty or materially closed the inequality gap between blacks and whites. (Between 1940 and 2000, black homeownership increased from 23 percent to 47 percent, still far lower than the 72 percent for whites, but a major increase, nonetheless.) For too many African Americans, dispossessed of their homes by the subprime mortgage catastrophe, homeownership has proved a cruel trap that has left them worse off than before. Without question, increased homeownership would increase the assets of a great many African Americans and help reduce the black/white gap in wealth. But as valuable as it is in the long run, equity in real estate does not provide the day-to-day income that buys food, purchases health insurance, or pays tuition bills. Jobs with wages high enough to pay a mortgage, backed by robust social insurance, are the prerequisites of both a decent life and secure homeownership. These are what far too many African Americans lack.

A focus on homeownership or, in fact, on any single factor, misses the two most important implications of the new African American inequality. First of all, because inequality is the result of a series of screens that filter African Americans into more- or less-favored statuses, policy interventions are needed at each of the crucial junctures. A fresh approach would identify policies designed to intervene at each point where circumstances threaten to propel African Americans through a screen that leaves them on the path toward more inequality and poverty. This approach requires an ambitious agenda that focuses simultaneously on neighborhood, school, and work as well as on the criminal justice and social welfare systems.

The second lesson from the recent history of African American inequality is this: in the last half of the twentieth century, institutions of the labor market and the state—a combination of vigorous government, active labor unions, a strong economy, and civil rights legislation—reduced black poverty, lessened the impact of discrimination, and moved many African Americans into the middle class. Today, by contrast, huge numbers of African American men remain outside the labor market, many in prison: poor African American women are pushed from welfare into low-wage work that offers scant hope of mobility; labor unions cover fewer workers; and the assault on government constricts the major source of black economic security and mobility. When they are injured on the job, blacks, like all American workers, face increasingly mean workers' compensation and unemployment programs. When they are sick, they are confronted with the well-documented limits of American health care. When they want to send their children to college, they encounter steeply rising tuitions at public universities. But the problems are not insuperable. Just because the engine of progress has stalled does not mean that it cannot be restarted. Nor are fiscal constraints an adequate excuse. The United States is a wealthy country that can pay for whatever it truly wants, whether waging an expensive war or subsidizing the very rich with tax breaks. Black poverty and inequality, in the last analysis, are problems of national imagination and will. Surmounting them requires understanding how they work today and finding the resolve to attack their sources. The task is difficult, but, then, the stakes are very high.

7

Latinos Face Discrimination Based on False Health Concerns

Geraldo Rivera

Geraldo Rivera hosts the television program Geraldo at Large *on* Fox News. *Rivera is a long-time television personality who began his career as a television reporter. Since then, he has worked on numerous shows, including ABC's* Good Morning America, *the* Geraldo Rivera Show, *and* Rivera Live. *He has won several awards, including the 2000 Robert F. Kennedy prize, the Peabody Award, and several Emmys for his work in journalism.*

Anti-immigrant activists draw connections between immigrants and disease in order to increase fear and panic among Americans, fanning the flames of anti-immigrant sentiment. Setting limits on immigration into the US based on the idea of maintaining America's ethnic balance, was often further justified in the early 1900s by anti-immigrant proponents who stressed fear about the spread of disease via immigrant populations. Similar sentiments are being stoked in recent immigrant debates—opponents of immigration point to illegal Hispanics as yet another reason that an already-dysfunctional public health system will eventually fail. They also continue to propagate false notions regarding lack of hygiene and health concerns among Hispanics to fan the flames of prejudice against them.

"The invasion of illegal aliens is threatening the health of many Americans," intoned Lou Dobbs gravely on his April 14, 2005, CNN program, as he led in to a report that made the alarming claim, "There were about nine hundred cases of leprosy for forty years. . . . There have been seven thousand in the past three years." The report's clear and specific intent was to convey the message that sick Mexicans and other aliens, but mostly Mexican migrants, are carrying fearsome diseases that are infecting thousands of innocent and otherwise healthy Americans. And that one result of this distressing phenomenon was a resurgence of this horrible disease that has haunted mankind since the biblical era. The new scourge was leprosy that was said to have been carried into America by aliens.

Fears About Immigrants and Disease

In May 2007 there was an awkward moment when CBS correspondent Leslie Stahl, in profiling Mr. Dobbs on *60 Minutes*, questioned him about the claim. The awkwardness was due to the fact that unknown to Stahl, the CNN anchor had just gotten a part-time job as a contributor to CBS's own *Early Show*.

Stahl said, "We checked that number and found a report issued by the federal government saying that seven thousand is the number of leprosy cases over the last thirty years, not the past three." Stahl added, "And nobody knows how many of those cases involve illegal immigrants."

"If we reported it, it's a fact," Dobbs answered with his customary arrogance. But it was not a fact, as the Southern Poverty Law Center (SPLC) demonstrated in interviews and in full-page ads in the *New York Times* and *USA Today* demanding a retraction of the inflammatory and false reporting. The fact is, leprosy "is not a public health problem—that's the bottom line," James Krahenbuhl, the director of the National Hansen's Disease Program, told the *New York Times* (Hansen's disease is the medical name for leprosy).

As *Times* reporter David Leonhardt proved, the Dobbs report was a lie, and if it were not for the specious connection to the debate on immigration, the CNN ace would never have reported it. He was wrong and unfair. Dobbs is also "one of the most popular people on the white supremacist Web sites," according to J. Richard Cohen, the CEO of the Southern Poverty Law Center, who told Dobbs to his face on a May 2007 broadcast, "You've got to ask yourself why the Council of Concerned Citizens considers you their favorite pundit." According to Cohen's colleague Mark Potok, "The anti-immigration movement is shot through with bigots, nuts and radicals like the Minutemen's Chris Simcox, who has been quoted as saying he saw elements of the Chinese army mobilizing on the Mexican border! Simcox has been an honored guest on Lou Dobbs's show at least twenty times." The hope at the SPLC is that the ridicule Dobbs received from other reporters, and even from both Jon Stewart and Stephen Colbert on Comedy Central, has dulled the CNN commentator's effectiveness. If so, it is long overdue.

As David Leonhardt put it in the *Times*:

> The problem with Mr. Dobbs is that he mixes opinion and untruths. He is the heir to the nativist tradition that has long used fiction and conspiracy theories as a weapon against the Irish, the Italians, the Chinese, the Jews and now, the Mexicans.

Historical Precedents

The connection between immigration and disease has long been used to generate distaste toward immigrants that sometimes borders on panic. And often the panic is accompanied by anti-immigrant violence. It is as predictable as the economic cycle of boom and bust. In May 1857, a quarantine facility on Staten Island, New York, designed to care for immigrants with contagious diseases like yellow fever, cholera, and smallpox, was burned to the ground by vigilantes concerned the new arrivals would spread disease to their community and suppress property values.

Another armed gang of thugs, who thankfully removed the patients first, burned a second facility the following September. When authorities could find no witnesses or evidence of responsibility for the arson, the *New York Times* reporter at the time wrote ... about vigilantism directed against immigrants being "deemed a pardonable offence."

There is not a speck of evidence suggesting that migrant farmworkers are any dirtier than native-born workers.

To be sure, in the era before effective public health, immigrants were sometimes a source of infectious disease, and they suffered an inevitable backlash when that was the case. In 1892, a cholera epidemic swept through New York, causing a tremendous antipathy toward the German immigrants who brought the disease with them on board a vessel out of Hamburg called the *Monrovia*. As quoted in *Coming to America*, the *New York Times* of all newspapers wrote in an August 29, 1892, front-page article:

> These people [immigrants] are offensive at best; under the present circumstances, they are a positive menace to the health of the country.... Cholera, it must be remembered, originates in the homes of this human riff-raff.

The whole concept of keeping out the "human riff-raff" became the central theme in America's immigration policy. The passage of the Immigration Act of 1924 capped total immigration at 150,000 a year and specifically set a limit of 2 percent of the population of each race already here. The idea of the racial quotas was to preserve America's ethnic "balance" by keeping out more immigrants from southern European countries, principally Italy, Spain, and Greece, and Slavic Eastern Europeans, who were thought genetically inferior to the nation's then WASP [White Anglo-Saxon Protestant] majority. Upon signing the bill into law, President Calvin Coolidge declared, "America must remain America."

And while immigration from the Mediterranean and Slavic peoples was severely curtailed, Africans were not even considered eligible to apply. The anti-immigration forces of the time also hyped fear of diseases like tuberculosis, using it not only to deport Mexican immigrants but also to "repatriate" back to Mexico some migrants who had already become citizens of the United States.

Many believe that it was the anti-immigrant mind-set and the fear of inferior races seeping into our society, as evidenced by the racist Chinese Exclusion Act of 1882 and the National Origins Act of 1924, as much as blatant anti-Semitism, that kept America from offering safe haven to Europe's doomed Jews on the eve of World War II.

In 1939, lobbied fiercely by his own anti-Semitic secretary of state, Cornell Hull, and flat-out threatened by a withdrawal of support in the coming election by southern Democrats, President Franklin D. Roosevelt was not exactly a profile in courage when he turned away the SS *St. Louis*, the infamous ship crammed with almost a thousand Jewish refugees. Their tragic "Voyage of the Damned" ended when the ship returned them to Europe on the eve of the Nazi invasion, where many of the ship's passengers perished.

Commentators of today are playing with the same tried and trusted handbook their predecessors used in the 1930s to justify President Herbert Hoover's policy of repatriation of immigrants, both those thought to have infectious diseases and even those who were healthy, but who it was feared might catch TB and then might need subsidized medical care. Their principal tactic is the generation of irrational fear of the worst kind, fear that close contact with these alien others can cause horrifying disease. The claims have little basis in fact, but the charge, once made, is difficult to rebut. Although leprosy is not the contemporary public health problem the Dobbs report wanted you to believe, a straw poll of Dobbs's viewers would probably indicate otherwise.

It was another bogeyman conjured to make a dishonest point. What will CNN blame the poor Mexicans for next? Venereal disease? Acne? Tooth decay?

Situation Today

Check out this article posted on the Americans for Legal Immigration PAC [political action committee] newsletter:

By Frosty

September 21, 2006

Why? As of Wednesday, 146 citizens in 23 states suffered E. Coli infection and one died. . . . How do you think this disease outbreak occurred? To bring it into sobering focus, please understand that 20 million illegal aliens crossed in to America in the past 20 years without any kind of health screening. They work picking our food, washing our dishes in restaurants and, as is the norm in Third World countries, rarely if ever wash their hands after using the toilet. Additionally, most of them suffer functional illiteracy. They do not practice personal hygiene or health habits most Americans assume as a normal aspect of living.

George Lopez and Carlos Mencia have a long-running feud over who thought up a joke that Frosty wouldn't find very funny. It goes something like: "You know who touches your Taco Bell before you do?" Then the joke gets really gross, detailing how migrant farm laborers can wreak havoc on hygiene to retaliate against societal abuse. It's only funny because it's *not* true. There is not a speck of evidence suggesting that migrant farmworkers are any dirtier than native-born workers. Ever been on a farm, Frosty? Did you bring wipes?

I have a great story about how a clever group of Cuban illegal migrants used the disease paranoia to gain entrance into the United States. In 2005, about forty of them were found at the Gateway International Bridge in Brownsville, Texas, a popular border crossing point. When they were apprehended by U.S. Customs agents, the group's spokesman told the agents they all had tuberculosis [TB]. The freaked-out agents then brought them into the United States, where everyone was chest X-rayed by nurses at the Cameron County Health Department. None had TB. Then, because of the unique law regarding Cuban refugees who touch American soil, all were permitted to stay. This is the Trojan Horse of the Cuban refugee saga.

There is one provable and ironic connection between Latino migrants and disease. Some of those who spent time in this country as seasonal workers are reportedly returning home to Mexico infected with HIV/AIDS they contracted in the United States. An eye-opening July 2007 report by Marc Lacey in the *New York Times* revealed an "expanding AIDS crisis among migrants [that] is largely overlooked on both sides of the border. . . . In the United States, it is often assumed that immigrants bring diseases into the country, not take them away." "They think that because it's the United States, [sex] is safer," Dr. Indiana Torres of the Puebla Mexico General Hospital told Lacey. "It's their fantasy and it's not true."

I bet you will never see this HIV/AIDS story reported by [Sean] Hannity, Dobbs, or [Michelle] Malkin. Stories have to fit their "illegal aliens are bad and bad for you" narrative to be worthy of comment, and their current theme is the imminent destruction of our way of life, famine, war, plague, and pestilence caused by rampant immigration.

8

The War on Terrorism Has Increased Bias Against Muslims

Peter W. Singer

Peter W. Singer is the director of the 21st Century Defense Initiative and a senior fellow in foreign policy at the Brookings Institution. His research focuses on issues of war, including U.S. defense needs and priorities. He has authored several books, including Corporate Warriors *and* Children at War.

Winning the war on terror is dependent on our ability to win the war of ideas. This is crucially important in the light of growing prejudice against Muslims, as evidenced in contemporary American political discourse and media coverage of Islam-related issues, which often link Muslims in general to extremist elements within the Islamic community. This prejudice compromises our national security, erodes our standing and goodwill among other nations of the world, and undermines the very principles of inclusiveness and acceptance that have helped sustain and grow American democracy.

Winning the war on terrorism depends on winning the war of ideas, perhaps even more so than during the Cold War. General David Petraeus, currently [2007] the top commander [of U.S. forces] in Iraq, once said that the war of ideas may be as much as 80 percent of the effort against extremists. Unfortunately, by most metrics, the United States is

Peter W. Singer, "American Goodwill, in Shackles," salon.com, June 26, 2007. This article first appeared in Salon.com, at http://www.salon.com. An online version remains in the Salon archives. Reprinted with permission.

losing this war, in Iraq and beyond. In a few short years, the United States has gone from being seen as the Cold War beacon on the hill of freedom, Coca-Cola and blue jeans to the dark home of Abu Ghraib, Guantanamo Bay and orange jumpsuits. Part and parcel of this failure has been a rising xenophobia and prejudice at home, undermining our efforts abroad.

Winning the War of Ideas

This war of ideas has been raised by almost all of the 2008 [U.S.] presidential campaigns. They have rightly discussed revitalizing our public diplomacy and making changes in foreign and security policies to restore American values. There even appears to be growing momentum inside the [George W.] Bush administration to close down Guantanamo [Bay detention center] though the debate is focused on legal issues in the wake of a Supreme Court ruling last year, rather than on the prison's undeniable corrosion of American prestige.

But there is a critical aspect of this debate that no current presidential contender has faced. While leaders like [Dwight] Eisenhower, JFK [John F. Kennedy], LBJ [Lyndon B. Johnson] and even [Richard] Nixon saw that we would never defeat the Soviet bloc in the Cold War battle of ideologies until we openly wrestled our deep problems with racism and civil rights at home, no candidate yet has wrestled with that period's 21st-century parallel. Just as it was hard to win hearts and minds in the Cold War battlegrounds of Africa and Asia as long as Jim Crow stood strong, it'll be impossible to win hearts and minds in the Muslim world as long as a vapid prejudice against Islam continues to grow in our political discourse and on our airwaves.

The deep and rapid deterioration of America's standing in the world is one of the greatest challenges the United States now faces. It took us most of the 20th century to build up a global reputation that melded both power and popularity, and yet we are squandering it away in the first years of the 21st century. The erosion of American credibility and standing in the world is not just some lost popularity contest. It alienates our allies and reinforces the recruiting efforts of our foes, and denies American ideas and policies a fair shake.

Shortly after [the terrorist attack of] 9/11, President Bush took the compelling step of visiting the Islamic Center of Washington, the capital's leading mosque, to show Americans and the world that the administration understood that the world's roughly 1.4 billion members of the Muslim faith were not to blame for the attacks carried out by a small set of murderers like [Osama] bin Laden. This week [June 2007], he goes back to the center for its rededication ceremony.

Islamic Xenophobia

Unfortunately, in the time between, the clarity of his message has been lost amid a politics of fear—a new sort of xenophobia, targeting the entire religion of Islam, as opposed to extremists within it, has become the norm. For example, a series of broad anti-Muslim statements has since been made by various U.S. officials and their close supporters, calling the religion of Islam "violent" and "evil." Rather than being refuted and condemned by senior officials, they were politely ignored. Illustrating the lack of costs that come with such expressions is the story of Lt. Gen. William G. Boykin, who in a 2003 speech compared his faith with a Muslim's by stating, "I knew that my God was bigger than his. I knew that my God was a real God and his was an idol." Boykin has since been promoted; today [2007] he is deputy undersecretary of defense for intelligence.

This quietly growing prejudice is not a right-left issue. Indeed, Michael Franc, vice president of government relations for the conservative Heritage Foundation, has warned of the dangers of "a real backlash against Islam" in the United States, noting that congressional leaders are exacerbating the problem by using language that links all Muslims with extremists.

Such discourse isn't only becoming acceptable in the political world, but is also being stoked in the mainstream of our media as well. For example, in 2005, Simon & Schuster published a book called *Sands of Empire*, by former *Wall Street Journal* correspondent Robert W. Merry. It was reviewed by all the major media. In it, Merry straightforwardly argued that "the enemy is Islam." Imagine if he had declared that "the enemy is Judaism" or "the enemy is the Blacks." Would it even have gotten published by a mainstream press, let alone promoted? Moreover, was he saying anything different than what you would hear on just five minutes of talk radio?

Today, a new prejudice undermines our national security, just as Jim Crow and images of police setting dogs upon civil rights protestors undermined our message of freedom some 40 years ago. At the heart of any discussion of the 21st-century war of ideas must be what former U.S. diplomat William Fisher recently warned of as an "uninformed and unreasoning Islamophobia that is rapidly become implanted in our national genetics." Indeed, a Gallup poll in 2006 found that only 49 percent of Americans believed U.S. Muslims are loyal to the United States and 44 percent believed that the entire religion of Islam itself is inherently extreme. Interestingly, six months after 9/11, the numbers were much lower—meaning that people had less prejudice back then, even while the pain was raw, than they do today. Likewise, in the 2006 poll, 39 percent advocated that all Muslims in the United States be required to carry a special ID.

Media's Influence and Bias

We need to remember that we live in an increasingly media-connected world, and demonstrations of prejudice at home resonate globally. Last year, the Brookings Institution (where I am a senior fellow), the Pew Forum and American University sponsored a student research team that went to nine countries and surveyed Muslim youth attitudes, drawing from more than 2,000 interviews. Whether it was in Turkey or Indonesia, the study found a consensus about how youth in the Muslim world—our key target audience in this war of ideas—think America regards them and their faith.

As one student researcher described of the interview results, "They think Americans just don't care and think all Muslims are evil or terrorists. They say, 'We get your media and see how you view Islam.'" Added another, "Wherever the group traveled, Fox News was on, and you'd see Ann Coulter calling people 'ragheads' over and over, or Glenn Beck on CNN."

The success of the Muslim and Arab-American communities is . . . definitive proof that the United States is not anti-Islam.

Beck is the same cable news "personality" who in a television interview asked Keith Ellison, the first Muslim to serve in Congress, "Sir, prove to me that you are not working with our enemies." Ellison equally was welcomed to the House of Representatives by Rep. Virgil Goode, a Republican from Virginia, who warned his constituents that Ellison's decision to use the Quran for his swearing-in was a threat to "the values and beliefs traditional to the United States of America."

Ellison illustrated the flaw in that sort of thinking by swearing his oath of office on a copy of the Quran that was originally owned by Thomas Jefferson. But the damage was done. While the attack on his patriotism echoed the same sort of questions about personal faith that plagued leaders like JFK [a Catholic] and now [2008 presidential candidate] Mitt Romney [a Mormon], it extends beyond mere electoral politics. What should have been a story to the Muslim world about the greatness and inclusiveness of American democracy instead became an illustration of how prejudice against Islam has become allowable in American discourse.

Tolerance and Acceptance

The saddest irony in all of this is that this trend is turning what should be our greatest strength into a weakness. The success of the Muslim and Arab-American communities is a remarkable demonstration of the opportunities afforded by the United States of America. The average income and education levels among Muslim and Arab Americans are higher than the national rates, a fact we should be announcing with fanfare in our public diplomacy—that is, if we had any. This is definitive proof that the United States is not anti-Islam, something that violent extremists like bin Laden often accuse us of being in their propaganda.

America provides a model of what citizenship and integration are all about, presenting an example that shines brightly compared with the autocratic regimes of the greater Middle East. The same is true with regard to the substandard treatment that many Muslims and Arabs face in Europe, which may be the future hub of homegrown terrorism. That America has a history of being the beacon on the hill is not merely something we should be proud of; its use is a strategic imperative. Yet we seem to be on a path to repeating the worst of our periods of prejudice of the 1960s, or even the 1940s.

We all know that hatemongering is un-American. But even more worrisome, it undermines our national security, endangering our ability to win the crucial war of ideas. Those wishing to become the next president must be asked how they will reverse this perilous trend.

9

School Desegregation Needs Improvement

Gary Orfield, Erica Frankenberg, and Liliana M. Garces

Gary Orfield is a professor at the University of California, Los Angeles, and also codirector of the Civil Rights Project/Proyecto Derechos Civiles. Erica Frankenberg and Liliana M. Garces are doctoral candidates at the Harvard University Graduate School of Education.

In 2007, the United States Supreme Court upheld the use of affirmative action policies in college admissions, allowing colleges and universities to continue the use of race as a factor in admission decisions. The victory is one-sided, though, because of the rising segregation trend in K–12 public schools. Research proves that segregated high schools with high minority populations consistently fail to prepare their students adequately for higher education; conversely, schools that service more affluent, white students fail to prepare their students to adjust to a diverse student body once they begin attending college. Segregation has been on the rise in American public schools for several decades—the main reasons for this increase are the limits placed on parental choice regarding which schools their children will attend, as well as the erosion of racial diversity guidelines in public schools. If this trend is not reversed, children from poorer, and often minority backgrounds, will continue to lag behind their more affluent peers. In the long run, increased segregation will place a heavier burden on colleges and universities as they struggle to provide equal educational access to students from diverse backgrounds. To pre-empt the negative effects of this trend, university faculty and education experts must help K–12 educators to maintain and actively encourage desegregation in public schools.

There was a national sigh of relief on campuses in June when an altered U.S. Supreme Court left standing the historic 2003 *Grutter v. Bollinger* decision supporting affirmation action in admissions. There had been widespread fear among civil rights advocates that a more conservative Supreme Court would seriously undermine or even reverse the 5-4 *Grutter* decision with its author, Justice Sandra Day O'Connor, no longer on the Court. The voluntary school integration decision in *Parents Involved in Community Schools v. Seattle School District No. 1* and *Meredith v. Jefferson County Board of Education* was, indeed, a serious reversal for desegregation in K–12 schools but while divided on the constitutionality of the school plans at issue in the cases, all nine justices agreed that the decision had no impact on the *Grutter* precedent. The rights of colleges to use race in admissions decisions for student body diversity had survived scrutiny by the most conservative Supreme Court in more than 70 years. Since the Supreme Court rarely takes such cases, the *Grutter* precedent might last for a while. While a bullet was dodged, optimism should be restrained. The dike protecting affirmative action has held but the river that brings diverse groups of students to colleges may be drying up as a result of the latest decision.

Affirmative Action in Colleges

Colleges and universities, especially selective institutions, tend to draw their successful minority applicants from interracial schools and their admissions offices know well that many of the segregated minority high schools fail to prepare their students well enough to succeed in college. Research by the Civil Rights Project has shown that too many segregated urban high schools are "dropout factories" where the main product is dropouts and successful preparation for college is rare. Conservative economist Eric Hanushek found that the damage was worst for the relatively high achieving black students, the very students likely to comprise the college eligible pool. So making segregation worse cuts the number of well prepared students. In addition to academic preparation, students from segregated backgrounds are also often not ready to function socially on a largely white, affluent campus. It also means of course, that the most segregated group of students in American schools, whites, also have less preparation to deal successfully with diversity. So colleges may have won, but also lost.

Districts that have ended the consideration of race as a criteria in their student assignment policies [predict] that race-neutral methods will lead to resegregation and growing inequality.

Even before the new decision, segregation had been on the rise for almost two decades in American public schools, partially as a result of three decisions by the Supreme Court limiting desegregation in the 1990s (*Board of Education of Oklahoma City v. Dowell, Freeman v. Pitts* and *Missouri v. Jenkins*). Because this new decision struck down the most common methods of creating integrated schools in districts without court orders to desegregate, it will likely precipitate further increases in segregation. Since 1980 the tools most commonly used to create integrated schools combine parental choice of schools with magnet programs and racial diversity guidelines. Now the limitations that prevented transfers and magnet choices that increased segregation are gone, and districts have to decide whether to do something more complex and multidimensional or abandon their integration efforts. It remains to be seen what will happen in various districts, of course, but the experience of other districts that have ended the consideration of race as a criteria in their student assignment policies suggests that race-neutral methods will lead to resegregation and growing inequality.

Research thus suggests that there are two significant implications for higher education to consider. First, rising segregation is likely to bring a rise in educational inequality and less prepared black and Latino students. Second, all incoming students are likely to have fewer interracial experiences prior to attending college meaning they will be less prepared for effective functioning in an interracial setting.

The Seattle and Louisville cases produced an outpouring of summaries of a half century of research by a number of groups of scholars. A subsequent review of the briefs by the non-partisan National Academy of Education confirms the central premise of *Brown v. Board of Education* that racially isolated minority schools offer students an inferior education, which is likely to harm their future life opportunities, such as graduation from high school and success in college. Racially isolated minority schools are often unequal to schools with higher percentages of white students in terms of tangible resources, such as qualified, experienced teachers and college preparatory curriculum, and intangible resources including low teacher turnover and more middle-class peers—all of which are associated with positive higher educational outcomes.

Minority students who graduate from integrated schools are more likely to have access to the social and professional networks normally available to middle class white students.

Although colleges and universities differ in their criteria and process for admissions, common elements to their admissions decisions for students include 1) whether a student has or will graduate from high school, 2) standardized test scores, and 3) number of advanced and Advanced Placement courses. Research consistently finds that minority students graduate at significantly lower rates in racially isolated minority schools; in fact, minority isolation is a significant predictor of low graduation rates, even when holding constant the effects of other school performance indicators. Academic achievement scores of students are also lower in segregated minority schools, and this effect can cumulate over time for students who spend multiple years attending segregated schools. Finally, many predominantly minority schools do not offer as extensive advanced curricular opportunities and levels of academic competition as do majority white or white and Asian schools.

The Impact of Diversity in Schools

In addition to offering different opportunities for academic preparation, research has also found that integrated schools offer minority students important connections to competitive higher education and information about these options. There are strong ties between successful high schools and selective colleges. Minority students who graduate from integrated schools are more likely to have access to the social and professional networks normally available to middle class white students. For example, a study of Latino students who excelled at elite higher educational institutions found that most students had attended desegregated schools—and gained academic confidence as well as critical knowledge about what they need to do to accomplish their aspirations (e.g., which courses to take from other, college-going students).

White students also lose if schools resegregate. Desegregation advocates assert that public school desegregation is powerful and essential because desegregated schools better prepare future citizens for a multiracial society. A critical component of this preparation is gaining the skills to work with people of diverse backgrounds. Segregated schools in segregated neighborhoods leave white as well and nonwhite students ill-prepared for what they will encounter in colleges and university classes or in their dorms.

Over 50 years ago, Harvard [University] psychologist Gordon Allport suggested that one of the essential conditions to reducing prejudice was that people needed to be in contact with one another, particularly under appropriate conditions. Research in racially integrated schools confirms that, by allowing for students of different races and ethnicities to be in contact with one another, students can develop improved cross-racial understanding and experience a reduction of racial prejudice and bias. Importantly, research suggests that other interventions such as studying about other groups are not as effective or as long-lasting as actually being in contact with students of other racial/ethnic backgrounds.

Research on graduates of racially integrated elementary and secondary schools has also found that students who graduated from these settings felt their integrated schooling experiences had better prepared them for college, including being more interested in attending integrated higher education institutions. The Civil Rights Project has surveyed high school juniors in a number of major school systems around the country and students in more diverse schools report feeling more comfortable living and working with others of different backgrounds than did their peers in segregated high schools.

The Future of Desegregation

As schools become more segregated, it will become more incumbent on colleges and universities to intensify their outreach and retention programs to improve access for all students, and to consider the extra burdens borne by the victims of segregation who have done nothing to deserve unequal opportunities. In particular, it will be critically important for colleges and universities to continue to use race in their outreach and retention programs. As colleges and universities that have sought to defend affirmative action policies have long understood and Justice Anthony M. Kennedy recently wrote, "The enduring hope is that race should not matter, the reality is that too often it does." Further, the need to help students understand how to productively live with others from diverse backgrounds will fall to higher education. As other institutions retreat from mirroring the racial diversity of our country, this may increasingly become a responsibility universities must shoulder.

Our incoming students already have more limited interracial experiences than the last generation of students, a trend that is likely to only get worse. We hope that many school districts will continue to value integration and seek more comprehensive policies under the new guidelines set forth in Justice Kennedy's controlling opinion, but it is very likely that segregation will worsen. We believe that university faculty and researchers who may have expertise to assist local school districts find legal and workable solutions to maintain diversity should offer support at this critical time. Universities can also take a public leadership and education role in continuing to argue for the importance of integrated educational settings. These actions could help limit some of the ill effects of the re-segregation of local schools and help keep alive the legacy of *Brown* in a period of judicial retreat.

10

Affirmative Action Should Be Changed

Peter H. Schuck

Peter H. Schuck is the Simeon E. Baldwin professor of law at Yale Law School. His major areas of research interest include tort law, immigration, citizenship, refugee law, and diversity. He has authored several books and writes regularly for the American Lawyer.

The role of affirmative action has changed dramatically over the last few decades. As it is currently defined and implemented, it no longer serves America well. Based on the wide-scale acceptance of the idea of nondiscrimination and the economic and social progress made by black Americans, current affirmative action policies must be abandoned in favor of general nondiscriminatory policies that allow for no preferential treatment in the public or private sector based on race. If needed, some private institutions could continue to use a modified affirmative action policy—in these cases, the application of these policies must be completely transparent and documented to ensure oversight. Due to the fact that nondiscrimination is now widely accepted as the norm, affirmative action, with its focus on race, only serves to highlight the importance of race in decisions that must begin to be based on merit. Although the moral foundation of affirmative action policies lay in the injustices suffered by black Americans and Native Americans, the dilution of the policy to accommodate other minorities has reduced the benefits

Peter H. Schuck, "Affirmative Action: Don't Mend It or End It—Bend It," *Brookings Review,* Winter 2002, pp. 24–27. Copyright © 2002 Brookings Institution. Reproduced by permission.

to blacks and Native Americans, the very people it was created to defend. Instead, Americans would be better served if we upheld our commitment to equal opportunity for all Americans, regardless of race and ethnicity.

Affirmative action's policy context has changed dramatically since 1970. One change is legal. Since the Supreme Court's 1978 [*University of California v.*] *Bakke* decision, when Justice Lewis Powell's pivotal fifth vote endorsed certain "diversity"-based preferences in higher education, the Court has made it increasingly difficult for affirmative action plans to pass constitutional muster unless they are carefully designed to remedy specific past acts of discrimination. Four other changes—the triumph of the nondiscrimination principle; blacks' large social gains; evidence on the size, beneficiaries, and consequences of preferences; and new demographic realities—persuade me that affirmative action as we know it should be abandoned even if it is held to be constitutional.

Nondiscrimination, or equal opportunity, is a principle questioned by only a few bigots and extreme libertarians.

"As we know it" is the essential qualifier in that sentence. I propose neither a wholesale ban on affirmative action ("ending" it) nor tweaks in its administration ("mending" it). Rather, I would make two structural changes to curtail existing preferences while strengthening the remaining ones' claim to justice. First, affirmative action would be banned in the public sector but allowed in the private sector. Second, private-sector institutions that use preferences would be required to disclose how and why they do so. These reforms would allow the use of preferences by private institutions that believe in them enough to disclose and defend them, while doing away with the obfuscation, duplicity, and lack of accountability that too often accompany preferences. Affirmative action could thus be localized and customized to suit the varying requirements of particular contexts and sponsors.

Triumph of the Nondiscrimination Principle

Why is change necessary? To explain, one must at the outset distinguish affirmative action entailing preferences from nondiscrimination, a principle that simply requires one to refrain from treating people differently because of their race, ethnicity, or other protected characteristics. Although this distinction can blur at the edges, it is clear and vital both in politics and in principle.

When affirmative action became federal policy in the late 1960s, the nondiscrimination principle, though fragile, was gaining strength. Preferences, by contrast, were flatly rejected by civil rights leaders like Hubert Humphrey, Ted Kennedy, and Martin Luther King, Jr. In the three decades that followed, more and more Americans came to embrace nondiscrimination and to oppose affirmative action, yet as John Skrentny shows in his *Ironies of Affirmative Action*, federal bureaucrats extended affirmative action with little public notice or debate. Today, nondiscrimination, or equal opportunity, is a principle questioned by only a few bigots and extreme libertarians, and civil rights law is far-reaching and remedially robust. In contrast, affirmative action is widely seen as a demand for favoritism or even equal outcomes.

Social Gains by Blacks

Blacks, the intended beneficiaries of affirmative action, are no longer the insular minority they were in the 1960s. Harvard sociologist Orlando Patterson shows their "astonishing" progress on almost every front. "A mere 13% of the population," he notes, "Afro-Americans dominate the nation's popular culture.... [A]t least 35 percent of Afro-American adult, male workers are solidly middle class." The income of young, intact black families approaches that of demographically similar whites. On almost every other social index (residential integration is a laggard), the black-white gap is narrowing significantly; indeed, the income gap for young black women has disappeared.

Even these comparisons understate black progress. Much of racism's cruel legacy is permanently impounded in the low education and income levels of older blacks who grew up under Jim Crow: their economic disadvantages pull down the averages, obscuring the gains of their far better-educated children and grandchildren. These gains, moreover, have coincided with the arrival of record numbers of immigrants who are competing with blacks. To ignore this factor, economist Robert Lerner says, is like analyzing inequality trends in Germany since 1990 without noting that it had absorbed an entire impoverished country, East Germany. In addition, comparisons that fail to age-adjust social statistics obscure the fact that blacks, whose average age is much lower than that of whites, are less likely to have reached their peak earning years.

My point, emphatically, is not that blacks have achieved social equality—far from it—but that the situation facing them today is altogether different than it was when affirmative action was adopted. Advocates, of course, say that this progress just proves that affirmative action is effective: hence it should be continued or even increased. But this *post hoc ergo propter hoc* [literally, "after this, therefore on account of this"] reasoning is fallacious and ignores the policy's growing incoherence and injustice.

Size, Beneficiaries, and Consequences of Preferences

When we weigh competing claims for scarce resources—jobs, admission to higher education, public and private contracts, broadcast or other spectrum licenses, credit, housing, and the like—how heavy is the thumb that affirmative action places on the scales? This is a crucial question. The larger the preference, the more it conflicts with competing interests and values, especially the ideal of merit—almost regardless of how one defines merit.

The best data concern higher education admissions where (for better or for worse) schools commonly use standardized test scores as a proxy for aptitude, preparation, and achievement. William Bowen and Derek Bok, the former presidents of Princeton and Harvard, published a study in 1999 based largely on the academic records of more than 80,000 students who entered 28 highly selective institutions in three different years. Affirmative action, they claimed, only applies to these institutions, although a more recent study suggests that the practice now extends to some second- and even third-tier schools.

Selective institutions, of course, take other factors into account besides race. Indeed, some whites who are admitted have worse academic credentials than the blacks admitted under preferences. Still, Bowen and Bok find a difference of almost 200 points in the average SAT [Standardized Achievement Test] scores of the black and white applicants, and even this understates the group difference. First, the deficit for black applicants' high school grade point average (GPA), the other main admission criterion, is even larger. Thomas Kane finds that black applicants to selective schools "enjoy an advantage equivalent to an increase of two-thirds of a point in [GPA]—on a four-point scale—or [the equivalent of] 400 points on the SAT." Second, although the SAT is often criticized as culturally biased against blacks, SAT (and GPA) scores at every level actually overpredict their college performance. Third, the odds were approximately even that black applicants with scores between 1100 and 1199 would be admitted, whereas the odds for whites did not reach that level until they had scores in the 1450–1499 range. With a score of 1500 or above, more than a third of whites were rejected while every single black gained admission. The University of Michigan, whose affirmative action program is detailed in a pending lawsuit, weighs race even more heavily than the average school in the Bowen and Bok sample. At Michigan, being black, Hispanic, or Native American gives one the equivalent of a full point of GPA; minority status can override any SAT score deficit. And a recent study of 47 public institutions found that the odds of a black student being admitted compared to a white student with the same SAT and GPA were 173 to 1 at Michigan and 177 to 1 at North Carolina State.

The moral case for affirmative action rests on the bitter legacy of black slavery, Jim Crow, and the violent dispossession of Native Americans.

These preferences, then, are not merely tie-breakers; they are huge—and they continue at the graduate and professional school levels. It is encouraging that an identical share (56 percent) of black and white graduates of the institutions in the Bowen and Bok sample earned graduate degrees; the share of blacks earning professional or doctoral degrees was actually slightly higher than for whites (40 percent vs. 37 percent). But black students' college grades and postgraduate test scores are so much lower on average that their admission to these programs, disproportionately at top-tier institutions, also depends on affirmative action. In the early 1990s, for example, only a few dozen of the 420 blacks admitted to the 18 most selective law schools would have been admitted absent affirmative action. A high percentage of these schools' black graduates eventually pass the bar examination, but some 22 percent of blacks from these schools who take the exam never pass it (compared with 3 percent of whites), and only 61 percent of blacks pass it the first time compared with 92 percent of whites. Blacks who enter the professions do enjoy solid status, income, civic participation and leadership, and career satisfaction. But this hardly makes the case for affirmative action, for the higher-scoring applicants whom they displaced would presumably have done at least as well.

How much of blacks' impressive gains is due to reduced discrimination resulting from changing white attitudes and civil rights enforcement, as distinct from preferences? How would they have fared had they attended the somewhat less prestigious schools they could have attended without preferences? What would the demographics of higher education be without those preferences? We cannot answer these vital questions conclusively. We know that black gains were substantial even before preferences were adopted, that preference beneficiaries are overwhelmingly from middle- and upper-class families, and that most black leaders in all walks of life did not go to elite universities. We also know that many institutions are so committed to affirmative action that they will find ways to prefer favored groups—minorities, legacies, athletes, and others—no matter what the formal rules say. Although California voters banned affirmative action in state programs, their politicians press the university system to jigger the admission criteria until it finds a formula that can skirt the ban and produce the "correct" number of the favored minorities (excluding Asians, who are thought not to need the help).

New Demographic Realities

The moral case for affirmative action rests on the bitter legacy of black slavery, Jim Crow, and the violent dispossession of Native Americans. Yet the descendants of slaves and Native Americans constitute a shrinking share of affirmative action's beneficiaries. Political logrolling has extended preferential treatment to the largest immigrant group, Hispanics, as well as to blacks from Africa, the Caribbean, and elsewhere, Asians and Pacific Islanders, and in some programs to women, a majority group.

Some affirmative action advocates acknowledge this problem and want to fix it. Orlando Patterson, for example, would exclude "first-generation persons of African ancestry" but not "their children and later generations . . . in light of the persistence of racist discrimination in America." He would also exclude all Hispanics except for Puerto Ricans and Mexican Americans of second or later generations and would exclude "all Asians except Chinese-Americans descended from pre-1923 immigrants. . . ." With due respect for Patterson's path-breaking work on race, his formula resembles a tax code provision governing depreciation expenses more than a workable formula for promoting social justice.

Centuries of immigration and intermarriage have rendered the conventional racial categories ever more meaningless. The number of Americans who consider themselves multiracial and who wish to be identified as such (if they must be racially identified at all) was 7 million in the 2000 census, including nearly 2 million blacks (5 percent of the black population) and 37 percent of all Native Americans. This is why advocacy groups who are desperate to retain the demographic status quo lobbied furiously to preempt a multiracial category.

In perhaps the most grimly ironic aspect of the new demographic dispensation, the government adopted something like the one-drop rule that helped enslave mulattos and self-identifying whites before Emancipation. Under OMB's [U.S. Office of Management and Budget] rules, any response combining one minority race and the white race must be allocated to the minority race. This, although 25 percent of those in the United States who describe themselves as both black and white consider themselves white, as do almost half of Asian-white people and more than 80 percent of Indian-white people. The lesson is clear: making our social policy pivot on the standard racial categories is both illogical and politically unsustainable.

Alternatives

Even a remote possibility that eliminating affirmative action would resegregate our society deeply distresses almost all Americans. Nothing else can explain the persistence of a policy that, contrary to basic American values, distributes valuable social resources according to skin color and surname. But to say that we must choose between perpetuating affirmative action and eliminating it entirely is false. To be sure, most suggested reforms—using social class or economic disadvantage rather than race, choosing among minimally qualified students by lottery, and making preferences temporary—are impracticable or would make matters worse. Limiting affirmative action to the descendants of slaves and Native Americans would minimize some objections to the policy but, as Patterson's proposal suggests, would be tricky to implement and would still violate the nondiscrimination and merit principles.

Race is perhaps the worst imaginable category around which to organize political and social relations.

Most Americans who favor affirmative action would probably concede that it fails to treat the underlying problem. Black applicants will continue to have worse academic credentials until they can attend better primary and secondary schools and receive the remediation they need. A root cause of their disadvantage is inferior schooling, and affirmative action is simply a poultice [temporary pain reliever]. We must often deal with symptoms rather than root causes because we do not know how to eliminate them, or consider it too costly to do so, or cannot muster the necessary political will. If we know which social or educational reforms can substantially improve low-income children's academic performance, then we should by all means adopt them. But this does not mean that we should preserve affirmative action until we can eliminate the root causes of inequality.

I propose instead that we treat governmental, legally mandated preferences differently than private, voluntary ones. While prohibiting the former (except in the narrow remedial context approved by the Supreme Court). I would permit the latter—but only under certain conditions discussed below. A liberal society committed to freedom and private autonomy has good reasons to maintain this difference; racial preferences imposed by law are pernicious in ways that private ones are not. To affirmative action advocates, it is a Catch-22 to bar the benign use of race now after having used it against minorities for centuries. But to most Americans (including many minorities), affirmative action is not benign. It is not a Catch-22 to recognize what history teaches—that race is perhaps the worst imaginable category around which to organize political and social relations. The social changes I have described only reinforce this lesson. A public law that affirms our common values should renounce the distributive use of race, not perpetuate it.

There are other differences between public and private affirmative action. A private preference speaks for and binds only those who adopt it and only for as long as they retain it. It does not serve, as public law should, as a social ideal. As I explained in *The Limits of Law: Essays on Democratic Governance,* legal rules tend to be cruder, more simplistic, slower to develop, and less contextualized than voluntary ones, which are tailored to more specific needs and situations. Legal rules reflect interest group politics or the vagaries of judicial decision; voluntary ones reflect the chooser's own assessment of private benefits and costs. Legal rules are more difficult to reform, abandon, or escape. Voluntary ones can assume more diverse forms than mandated ones, a diversity that facilitates social learning and problem solving.

Still, many who believe in nondiscrimination and merit and who conscientiously weigh the competing values still support affirmative action. If a private university chooses to sacrifice some level of academic performance to gain greater racial diversity and whatever educational or other values it thinks diversity will bring, 1 cannot say—nor should the law say—that its choice is impermissible. Because even private affirmative action violates the nondiscrimination principle, however, I would permit it only on two conditions: transparency and protection of minorities. First, the preference—its criteria, weights, and reasons—must be fully disclosed. If it cannot withstand public criticism, it should be scrapped. The goal is to discipline preferences by forcing institutions to reveal their value choices. This will trigger market, reputational, and other informal mechanisms that make them bear more of the policy's costs rather than just shifting them surreptitiously to nonpreferred applicants, as they do now. Second, private affirmative action must not disadvantage a group to which the Constitution affords heightened protection. A preference favoring whites, for example, would violate this condition.

The Commitment to Legal Equality

For better *and* for worse, American culture remains highly individualistic in its values and premises, even at some sacrifice (where sacrifice is necessary) to its goal of substantive equality. The illiberal strands in our tangled history that enslaved, excluded, and subordinated individuals as members of racial groups should chasten our efforts to use race as a distributive criterion. Affirmative action in its current form, however well-intended, violates the distinctive, deeply engrained cultural and moral commitments to legal equality, private autonomy, and enhanced opportunity that have served Americans well—even though they have not yet served all of us equally well.

11

Science Is Sometimes Used to Justify Racism

William H. Tucker

William H. Tucker is professor of psychology at Rutgers University and specializes in the study of social scientists whose work is used to support oppressive social policies. Tucker has published several books on the subject of race science, including The Funding of Scientific Racism.

Racism is a result of the disparity between beliefs about freedom and equality juxtaposed with the exclusionary treatment meted out to specific minorities. Societies that exhibit systematic racism often use science and principles of rational thought to justify its existence. Three broad scientific explanations have been proffered to justify racism: the notion that biological disaster would result from racial interbreeding, resulting in legal restrictions against interracial marriages; genetic differences between races would result in offspring afflicted with genetic aberrations or inferior mental and physical characteristics; and the claim that some ethnic groups are genetically inferior to others. Although these ideas no longer have widespread acceptance among modern scientists, these claims must be stringently rejected to move modern discussions of race and prejudice forward.

In his exceptionally insightful book, *Racism: A Short History*, Stanford University historian George M. Fredrickson notes the paradox that notions of human equality were the neces-

William H. Tucker, "The Ideology of Racism: Misusing Science to Justify Racial Discrimination," *United Nations Chronicle*, 2007, pp. 18–19. Copyright © 2007 United Nations. Reprinted with the permission of the United Nations.

sary precondition to the emergence of racism. If a society is premised on an assumption of inequality, producing an accepted hierarchy—one unquestioned even by those relegated to its nadir [lowest point]—then there is no need to locate the cause of the underlings' position in some specific characteristic on their part that makes them less worthy than others.

The Rise of Racism

However, as societies have become increasingly committed to the belief in freedom and equality—as once revolutionary ideas about equal rights for all have become more widespread, especially in the West—then those groups that are systematically denied these entitlements are claimed to possess what Fredrickson calls "some extraordinary deficiency that makes them less than fully human". That is, racism arose as a result of the contradiction between egalitarian principles coupled with the exclusionary treatment of specific ethnic groups: the rejection of organically hierarchical societies brought with it the implied necessity to account for the fact that some groups were subjected to servitude, enforced separation from the rest of society, or ghettoization. Beginning around the end of the eighteenth century, as Enlightenment rationalism replaced faith and superstition as the source of authority, the pronouncements of science became the preferred method for reconciling the difference between principle and practice. In societies in which there has been systematic discrimination against specific racial groups, inevitably it has been accompanied by attempts to justify such policies on scientific grounds.

Science and Racism

Broadly speaking, there have been three types of scientific explanations offered in putative support for racial discrimination, each of them having a lengthy history. One approach has been to claim that there are biological dangers involved in racial interbreeding. Indeed, it was precisely on the basis of this belief that in the United States and South Africa for many years there were statutory prohibitions against intermarriage. The first supposed evidence for this conclusion was provided in the mid-nineteenth century primarily by physicians, who claimed that, as a result of their mixed blood, "mulattoes" were considerably more susceptible to disease than either of their parents and thus exceptionally short-lived. In addition, were persons of mixed race to intermarry, according to leading anthropologists at the time, they became progressively less fertile, eventually becoming completely sterile.

Science has been used to support racial discrimination ... through pronouncements that some groups are systematically less well endowed than others in important cognitive or behavioural traits.

In the early twentieth century, shortly after the scientific community's discovery of Gregor Mendel's work led to a new, exciting branch of biology, geneticists warned that the intermarriage of "far apart" races could produce what they called genetic "disharmonies". Charles Benedict Davenport, a world renowned researcher at the time, observed, for example, that if a member of a tall race, such as the Scots, should mate with a member of a small race, such as the Southern Italians, their offspring could inherit the genes for large internal organs from one parent and for small stature from the other, resulting in viscera that would be too large for the frame. Naturally these claims were not tenable for long, but they were soon replaced by assertions less easily disprovable, as some social scientists insisted that the children of mixed race parentage were morally and intellectually inferior to either of the parents.

Although belief in such genetic mismatches was once fairly widespread within the scientific community and cited specifically to rationalize various racially oppressive policies, this notion now enjoys far less credibility. However, while there has been absolutely no evidence that racial interbreeding can produce a disharmony of any kind, warnings of some kind of genetic discord are still far from entirely extinct. Only a few years ago, Glayde Whitney, a prominent geneticist and former president of the Behavior Genetics Association, claimed that the intermarriage of "distant races" could produce a harmful genetic mixture in offspring, citing the wide range of health problems afflicting African Americans and their high infant death rate as examples of the effects of "hybrid incompatibilities" caused by white genes that were undetected due to the "one drop" convention defining all "hybrids" as blacks. Unsurprisingly, he was also a regular speaker before neo-Nazi groups and, in an address to a convention of Holocaust deniers, blamed Jews for a conspiracy to weaken whites by persuading them to extend political equality to blacks.

Another trend in the scientific justification of racial discrimination has been the claim that prejudice is a natural and indeed an essential phenomenon necessary for the evolutionary process to be effective by ensuring the integrity of gene pools. In this view, evolution exerts its selective effect not on individuals but on groups, which makes it necessary for races to be kept separate from each other and relatively homogeneous if there is to be evolutionary progress. One anthropologist who adheres to this belief refers to the tendency to "distrust and repel" members of other races as a natural part of the human personality and one of the basic pillars of civilization.

Driving Division Home

Finally, the most common way in which science has been used to support racial discrimination is through pronouncements that some groups are systematically less well endowed than others in important cognitive or behavioural traits. This is not to say that there may be no group differences in these traits, but rather that at this point there are no clear conclusions, which in any event would be irrelevant to issues of social and political equality. Nevertheless, there is again a long history of the use of such claims for oppressive purposes. For the first quarter of the twentieth century, there was particular concern over the results of early intelligence tests, which supposedly demonstrated that Southern and Eastern Europeans were not only intellectually inferior to their Northern counterparts, but were also unfit for self-rule. Some of the most important scientists of the time explained that Nordics, characterized as they were by greater self-assertiveness and determination, as well as intelligence, were destined by their genetic nature to rule over other races. In the last half century, the controversy over intellectual and moral traits has focused primarily on the differences between blacks and other races, which were often cited by those seeking to preserve white minority rule in South Africa and legal segregation in the United States.

At present, the most well known researcher to emphasize the importance of racial differences is Canadian psychologist J. Philippe Rushton, the author of *Race, Evolution, and Behavior: A Life History Perspective*, which was distributed unsolicited in an abridged version to tens of thousands of social scientists in an unsubtle attempt to influence both fellow scientists and public opinion. In the preface to the abridged paperback, Rushton promised to explain why races differ in crime rates, learning ability and AIDS prevalence. In the ensuing account, he asserted that the behaviour of blacks, whether in Africa or the diaspora, reflected what he called a "basic law of evolution", in which reproductive strategy was linked to intellectual development, such that the more advanced the latter, the fewer the number of offspring and the greater the investment of time and effort in the care of each of them. Thus, he declared, in comparison to Caucasians and Asians, blacks tended to be more sexually active and aggressive, while less intelligent and less capable of self-control, complex social organization and family stability. Like Glayde Whitney, Rushton too has been a favourite speaker at conventions of organizations dedicated to political policies that would encode white supremacy officially into law.

In the aftermath of the Second World War, two conferences of internationally recognized scientists, held by the United Nations, Educational, Scientific and Cultural Organization (UNESCO), issued statements about race. Although there were some slight differences in their observations about the possibility of innate differences, both groups agreed that equality as an ethical principle concerning the rights to be enjoyed by all members of a society was not predicated on any scientific conclusion about racial characteristics. This position should still inform our thinking about race and science. Although the strains of thought discussed in this article do not have widespread support among contemporary scientists, whether they are appropriate issues for scientific pursuit is beside the point. Such claims, scientifically bogus, or valid, should be utterly irrelevant to the entitlements enshrined in the UN Universal Declaration of Human Rights.

12

Reparations for African Americans Must Move Forward

Crystal L. Keels

Crystal L. Keels is a writer for Black Issues in Higher Education.

Historically, Americans have ignored the issue of accountability and reparation to black Americans for injustices suffered due to slavery and segregation. However, the issue is becoming harder to avoid because many activists continue to bring attention to it. Although recent events, including several convictions of criminals resulting from decades-old hate crimes and a 2005 apology by the U.S. Senate about the crime of lynching are positive happenings, apologies are insufficient, and a solid plan for restitution is needed. Activists working toward the goal of formal restitution sometimes explain that part of the resistance stems from ignorance—there is a lack of understanding among American legislators about the extent of damage done to African Americans over the years based on racial discrimination, slavery, and other oppressive practices. We need to recognize, however, that there is genuine resistance to reparation for black Americans, despite the fact that there is precedent for such a system of justice. The U.S. government has already made amends to Native Americans who lost land by paying over $1 billion in compensation, plus 4 million acres of land; Japanese Americans interred during World War II also received reparation for their ill treatment; and across

Crystal L. Keels, "Still No 40 Acres, Still No Mule," *Black Issues in Higher Education*, vol. 22, August 11, 2005, pp. 18–21. Copyright © 2005 Cox, Matthews & Associates. Reproduced by permission.

the world, millions of victims of the Jewish Holocaust have received compensation. The idea of compensation for African Americans remains a contentious issue—yet, it is one that the country must face and address.

The simple mention of reparations for African-Americans in the United States can be counted on to generate a firestorm. When it comes to the issue of recompense for injustices Black Americans have suffered throughout U.S. history—slavery, Jim Crow segregation and other political and social mechanisms designed to maintain racial inequality—the question of accountability is one the nation has historically ignored. The United States has customarily denied the need for restitution for the "peculiar institution" of slavery and its aftemath, and the legendary post–Civil War promise of "40 acres and a mule" still remains elusive.

But in the 21st century, avoiding the issue is becoming increasingly difficult as activists, scholars, politicians and grass-roots organizations work diligently to ensure that the issue of reparations for African-Americans and all people of African descent is one the country—indeed the world—must at least consider.

Acknowledgements and Apologies

A spate of recent public apologies for connections to the crime of slavery and other racial injustices have surprised many, considering a cultural context that for centuries maintained an adamant disavowal of responsibility for the degradation of millions of people of African descent.

"We are beginning to look back and correct the past," says Harvard law professor Charles J. Ogletree, Jr. "The good news is that things we never imagined would happen last year happened." He notes this year's [2005] conviction of Edgar Ray Killen for the 1964 murders of civil rights workers James Earl Chaney, Andrew Goodwin and Michael Schwerner; the reinvestigation of the 1955 kidnapping, torture and murder of 14-year-old Emmett Till; and the recent apology for the crime of lynching issued by the U.S. Senate. "These are major steps," he says.

In mid-July [2005], a South Carolina church service was held to atone for the 1916 lynching of a wealthy Black farmer who was hung from a pine tree and shot to death by a White mob after a quarrel with a White man over the price of cotton. And in June, Wachovia Corporation, the North Carolina-based financial giant, offered an apology for its historical ties to slavery. Other modern banking and insurance companies, including JPMorgan Chase, have come under public scrutiny for their involvement in the highly profitable slave trade.

The Wachovia findings were the result of a Chicago city ordinance supported by Alderwoman Dorothy Tillman, a project that Ogletree has been instrumental in as part of the Reparations Coordinating Committee. City law requires that companies that want to do business with the city of Chicago disclose any historical ties to slavery. In compliance with that ordinance, Wachovia uncovered its links to slavery through past acquisitions of institutions that owned enslaved Black people.

"We are deeply saddened by these findings," Wachovia chairman and CEO Ken Thompson said in a statement. "On behalf of Wachovia Corporation, I apologize to all Americans, especially African-Americans and people of African descent."

An apology is not nearly enough—some type of restitution must be made.

Public response to these events demonstrates that admissions and acknowledgements are not necessarily welcome news, however. John Carlisle, director of policy at the National and Legal Policy Center, a conservative organization dedicated to "promoting ethics in public life," said in a recent article that in Wachovia's case, an apology is "ridiculous" and adds that "slavery reparations is nothing but a shakedown, pure and simple." Carlisle argues that the company was mistaken to take responsibility "for business transactions conducted more than a century and a half ago," and has now opened itself up to possible lawsuits. Conservative columnist Thomas Sowell, senior fellow at the Hoover Institution, similarly describes reparations as a "hustle."

And some contend that an apology is all that is necessary. Dr. Carol M. Swain, professor of political science and law at Vanderbilt University, said in a recent article in the *Washington Post* that a national apology for slavery is sufficient to "bring closure and healing to a festering wound" and would not leave the government liable for monetary redress.

Still others argue that an apology is not nearly enough—some type of restitution must be made.

Ogletree is not alone in his quest for redress. Notable supporters of reparations include James Lloyd; Alfred L. Brophy; Michele Roberts; Kimberly Ellis; Randall Robinson, author of *The Debt: What America Owes to Blacks* and founder of the TransAfrica Forum; Dennis Sweet; Adjoa Aiyetoro; Eric J. Miller; Sharon Cole; and James O. Goodwin, members of the Reparations Coordinating Committee.

Although the U.S. Supreme Court brief Ogletree and others filed in March 2005 on behalf of the survivors of the 1921 race riots in Tulsa, Okla., was denied in May [2005], he sees this as a long-term effort, and one he considers a way to give back, he says, for the benefits he and others received from the *Brown vs. Board of Education* ruling that made segregation unconstitutional.

Ogletree is working on behalf of the more than 100 living survivors of the race riot during which 300 people died and a thriving Black business district and hundreds of Black homes were destroyed. "This is a marathon, not a sprint to bring some true relief in Tulsa," Ogletree says.

A Contentious Issue

Ogletree adds that a significant aspect of the movement toward reparations is an educational one—even for elected officials.

"When we held our hearings, it was amazing how many in Congress didn't know the story (of the 1921 Tulsa race riots)," he says.

There are precedents . . . to consider and quantify what was taken from African-Americans and others in the form of labor without appropriate compensation.

Bringing the facts to light is a major motive behind HR40, the Commission to Study Reparations Proposals for African Americans Act. The bill was first introduced in Congress in 1989 by U.S. Rep. John Conyers, Jr., D-Mich., but has met with great resistance and has yet to pass.

The precedent for reparations for past injustices against other ethnic groups in this country has been set. On the Millions for Reparations Web site, Dr. Raymond Winbush, director of the Urban Institute at Morgan State University in Baltimore, notes that the United States in 1971 paid reparations of $1 billion plus 4 million acres of land for the Alaska Natives Land Settlement; in 1980, $81 million for the Klamath tribes of Oregon; in 1985, $105 million for the Lakota people of South Dakota; and in 1988 the govemment paid $1.2 billion for the Civil Liberties Act for Japanese Americans interred during World War II. And on a global scale, victims of the Jewish Holocaust have received hundreds of millions of dollars. But the notion of reparations for African-Americans remains a highly contentious issue.

"This is a legal issue," says Adam Clayton Powell III, director of the Integrated Media Systems Center and a visiting professor at the University of Southern California. "There are precedents, notably the treatment of assets taken by Nazis from Jews and some other victims. It may be uncomfortable for those of us in the U.S. to consider appropriate compensation for what was taken from American Indians—Hawaii is providing a case in point right now—and to consider and quantify what was taken from African-Americans and others in the form of labor without appropriate compensation," Powell says.

"The issue itself at the very least seeks to provide remedies that hold the prospects for equalizing life chances in this country for African-Americans," says Dr. Marvin Haire, associate director of research and publications for the Delta Research and Cultural Institute at Mississippi Valley State University, and former president and current member of the National Conference of Black Political Scientists. "There are some people who still claim African-American inferiority that is rooted in slavery. As long as those notions continue to exist, this will remain a contentious issue," he says.

Dr. Tyrone Simpson, assistant professor of English and urban studies at Vassar College, echoes similar sentiments. "The underlying logic historically of Black attempts to gain full citizenship within American society embraced by both Black and non-Black thinkers is that somehow Black people have to earn their citizenship," he says. "That in some way moral virtue is a prerequisite for protections from the state. That is an illusion that has been socially created. It is not a legal requirement," Simpson says.

Ida Hakim, founder of Caucasians United for Reparations and Emancipation [CURE] which in June [2005] held its second national convention in Atlanta, was motivated to create the organization after witnessing the ways in which her husband, a Black man, experiences the notion of African-American inferiority in his daily life.

"I saw what he encountered on a daily basis. I had to find out what I could do—what White people could do—to make amends," Hakim says. She says she contacted Silis Muhammad, chairman of the board of All for Reparations and Emancipation, and founder of the National Commission on Reparations, who suggested she support African-American reparations.

"I hadn't heard of it before and began to investigate. I felt reparations was an idea that would make me very unpopular. I thought, 'They are going to hate me,'" Hakim recalls. "But I decided to go ahead anyway." Hakim says she wrote letters to editors as a way to start, and CURE has now been in existence for 14 years.

"This is the right thing," she says. "White people are way off base with their knee-jerk reactions (to the issue)." She notes the deep-seated racism that exists in the United States and says CURE encounters all types of opposition. "We stress the advantages of creating a climate of justice," she says. "It is a war that has to be won one mind at a time."

It is not just White minds that resist the notion of African-American reparations, however, says Dr. Manning Marable, professor of public affairs, political science, history and African-American studies at Columbia University in New York City, and founding director of the Columbia University Institute for Research in African-American Studies. "Part of the public affairs work is to convince Black people that compensation is deserved," Marable explains. "This is no handout. Trillions of dollars have been given to Whites for hundreds of years." He points to Halliburton and other contemporary instances where preferential treatment is given to increase White wealth. "This is racialized," he says. "Blacks and people of color are nowhere to be found. And this reinforces economic disparities." He adds that the U.S. government is responsible for crimes against American Indians and, in kind, the call for African-American reparations is justified. "Black people should never be apologetic," Marable says.

"It's a matter of justice," says Winbush. "Justice is not a handout."

Next Steps

The notion of individual reparations has become almost a moot point, except in a few cases, primarily because the enslaved and their direct descendents are no longer living. But many Black soldiers who served during World War II and came home to a segregated world are.

"We should focus on reparations for World War II veterans who couldn't use the GI Bill to its fullest extent" says Dr. Richard Pierce, associate professor of history and chair of Africana studies at Notre Dame. "One could track the loss of income they could have received." He explains that often, Black veterans were limited in the choices they could make for housing and education because of segregation. "In these areas the government capitulated to existing social codes. The veterans are still alive and the government is culpable."

Reparations is about the redistribution of wealth and power and about changing well-entrenched beliefs. That change will not come easily or cheaply.

Marable makes a similar assertion and argues that the GI Bill served as "affirmative action for millions of working-class Whites to become middle class." He notes that the federal government transferred billions of dollars to make this social transformation possible. "When White baby boomers die they will leave their children and grandchildren $7 trillion in wealth. Black baby boomers will leave debt," he says, based on 2001 figures. "One out of three Black households actually has a negative net wealth."

It is this lack of wealth and infrastructure that needs to be addressed, says Dr. Haki Madhubuti, distinguished professor and director of the Master of Fine Arts in Creative Writing Program at Chicago State University.

"Money stays within the Black community for four hours, so whatever money comes in, goes out," Madhubuti says. He recommends that the establishment of independent Black institutions at "every level of human involvement" is necessary. "If this country wants to reinvigorate the economy, in order for us to put ourselves in competition, we have to have wealth creation," Madhubuti says.

Many of those in favor of reparations say such wealth creation or transfer of wealth will have to occur on the global stage, because of continuing resistance in the United States, and is also necessary to keep the nation globally competitive.

"The problem historically with American leaders who have thought to address the wrong of slavery is that they have always tried to do it without causing the state or its population some type of economic discomfort or inconvenience," says Vassar's Simpson. "In the same way the government has invested in Whiteness in mid-century, to equalize the playing field it is only decent that they invest in Blackness at this present time," he says. "One way to invest would be to over-invest, to designate the lion's share of local city, state and federal budgets in education in the direction of urban schools where Black children are most inclined to be enrolled."

Alfred Brophy, professor of law at the University of Alabama, which also recently disclosed its extensive ties to slavery, says that real change is a challenge. He notes that one of Thomas Jefferson's followers in a debate in the Virginia legislature in the 1820s asked the question, "When were men in power ever ready for reform?" "Almost never," Brophy says. "Reparations is about the redistribution of wealth and power and about changing well-entrenched beliefs. That change will not come easily or cheaply."

Continuing research, legal action and organizing at various levels will maintain the momentum behind movements towards African-American reparations, which Winbush says have accelerated since 2002, as activists regrouped after Sept. 11. He says the extent of the growing interest in reparations is demonstrated by the recent workshops on the topic held during the 2005 national NAACP convention in Milwaukee, and represents a major breakthrough for the issue of African-American reparations, which has historically been relegated to the margins of the U.S. mainstream.

"Very clearly, once we pull these issues out, air these issues and put them in the proper context of truth and fact then we can move toward reconciliation," says Hilary Shelton, director of the NAACP [National Association for the Advancement of Colored People] Washington Bureau Government Affairs Office. Shelton says the NAACP's official stance is to support HR40 and its goal to create a federal study commissioned to assess the damage done and then craft recommendations to address possible means of restitution. "Some people say let sleeping dogs lie, but at some point that sleeping dog is going to wake up. We are going to have to move toward healing—social justice and what that means—through an organized and clear judicious process," he says. "It needs to happen."

Says Marable: "We have to push forward to fight this with international law. In Africa, debt forgiveness, waiving the debt, a transfer of wealth from the West—it's the same issue. Africa is an economic basket case because of slavery and colonialism," he says. "[British Prime Minister] Tony Blair is forcing the issue in the European Union. We ought to be pushing that agenda here."

Organizations to Contact

The editors have compiled the following list of organizations concerned with the issues presented in this book. The descriptions are derived from materials provided by the organizations. The list was compiled on the date of publication of the present volume; the information provided here may change. Be aware that many organizations take several weeks or longer to respond to inquiries, so allow as much time as possible.

American Civil Liberties Union
125 Broad Street, 18th Floor, New York, NY   10004
(212) 549-2500 • fax: (212) 549-2646
Web site: www.aclu.org

The American Civil Liberties Union (ACLU) is a national organization that works to defend Americans' civil rights as guaranteed by the U.S. Constitution. The ACLU focuses on preserving First Amendment rights, including freedom of speech, freedom of the press, and freedom of religion; promoting the right to equal protection under the law; and preserving the right to privacy against unwarranted government intrusion.

American Immigration Control Foundation
P.O. Box 525, Monterey, VA   24465
(540) 468-2022 • fax: (540) 468-2024
Web site: www.aicfoundation.com

The American Immigration Control Foundation is a research and educational organization whose primary goal is to promote a reasonable immigration policy based on national interests and needs. The foundation educates the public on the negative effects of uncontrolled immigration. It publishes the monthly newsletter Border Watch as well as several monographs and books on the historical, legal, and demographic aspects of immigration.

Anti-Defamation League
605 Third Avenue, New York, NY   10158-3560
(212) 885-7951 • fax: (212) 885-5855
Web site: www.adl.org

The Anti-Defamation League (ADL), founded in 1913, is the world's leading organization fighting anti-Semitism through information, education, legislation, and advocacy. The ADL Materials Resource Center offers extensive materials on prejudice, discrimination, ethnicity, stereotyping, and scapegoating. It also offers other tools designed to help schools and communities teach and learn about diversity and enhance understanding of different groups. The ADL Education Division and its A World of Difference Institute offer prejudice-reduction training for schools, colleges and universities, the workplace, and the community.

Citizens' Commission on Civil Rights
2000 M Street NW, Suite 400, Washington, DC   20036
(202) 659-5565 • fax: (202) 223-5302
e-mail: citizen@cccr.org
Web site: www.cccr.org

Citizens' Commission on Civil Rights (CCCR) is a bipartisan organization that monitors the civil rights policies and practices of the federal government, based on the belief that the civil rights agenda must benefit the entire nation and not just specific interest groups. CCCR is a primary source of information and data regarding federal civil rights progress in the areas of housing equality, voting, and affirmative action.

Center for the Study of White American Culture
245 West 4th Avenue, Roselle, NJ   07203
(908) 241-5439 • fax: (908) 245-4972
e-mail: contact@euroamerican.org
Web site: www.euroamerican.org

The Center for the Study of White American Culture supports cultural exploration and self-discovery among white Americans. It encourages a dialogue among all racial and cultural groups concerning the role of white American culture in the larger American society.

Educators for Social Responsibility
23 Garden Street, Cambridge, MA   02138
(800) 370-2515 • fax: (617) 864-5164
e-mail: educators@esrnational.org
Web site: www.esrnational.org

Educators for Social Responsibility (ESR) works directly with educators to create and implement systemic practices that create safe and equitable schools for students of all backgrounds. ESR is a leading national center for staff development, school improvement, curricular resources, and support for schools, families, and children. ESR works with adults to advance teaching social responsibility as a core practice in the schooling and upbringing of children. ESR is recognized nationally for its leadership in conflict resolution, violence prevention, intergroup relations, and character education. The Resolving Conflict Creatively Program, an initiative of ESR, is one of the largest and longest-running programs in conflict resolution and intergroup relations in the country.

Hope in the Cities
2201 West Broad Street, Suite 200, Richmond, VA   23220
(804) 358-1764 • fax: (804) 358-1769
Web site: www.hopeinthecities.org

Hope in the Cities is an interracial, multifaith national network that seeks to encourage a process of healing through honest conversations on race, reconciliation, and responsibility. It focuses specifically on the acknowledgment and healing of racial history, the sustaining of dialogues involving people of all races and viewpoints, and the acceptance of personal responsibility for the process of change. Hope in the Cities assists communities in the United States and abroad to build diverse coalitions with people in business, government, media, education, and religious and community organizations.

National Association for the Advancement of Colored People (NAACP)

4805 Mount Hope Drive, Baltimore, MD   21215
(877) NAACP-98
Web site: www.naacp.org

Founded in 1909, the NAACP is one of the oldest and most influential civil rights groups in the United States. Throughout its existence it has worked primarily through the legal system on behalf of the rights of African Americans, but its goal is to ensure the political, educational, social, and economic equality of rights of all persons and to eliminate racial hatred and racial discrimination. Since 1910, the NAACP has published *The Crisis*, a magazine is dedicated to discussing critical issues confronting people of color, American society, and the world in addition to highlighting the historical and cultural achievements of diverse people.

National Council of La Raza

1126 16th Street, NW, Washington, DC   20036
(202) 785-1670 • fax: (212) 344-5332
e-mail: comments@nclr.org
Web site: www.nclr.org

The National Council of La Raza (NCLR), the largest national Hispanic civil rights and advocacy organization in the United States, works to improve opportunities for Hispanic Americans. NCLR conducts applied research, policy analysis, and advocacy, providing a Latino perspective in five areas—assets and investments, civil rights and immigration, education, employment and economic status, and health. It produces research reports and more general publications on issues such as health care, poverty, immigration, civil rights, and education.

National MultiCultural Institute

3000 Connecticut Avenue NW, Suite 438
Washington, DC   20007
(202) 483-0700 • fax: (202) 483-5233

e-mail: nmci@nmci.org
Web site: www.nmci.org

The National MultiCultural Institute (NMCI) is a private, nonprofit organization founded in 1983 to promote understanding and respect among people of different racial, ethnic, and cultural backgrounds. NMCI provides a forum for discussing the critical issues of multiculturalism through biannual conferences, diversity training and consulting, special projects, resource materials, and a multilingual mental health referral network. NMCI provides training and technical assistance on all aspects of organizing and facilitating dialogue groups.

Project Change
4110 Redwood Road, Suite 351, Oakland, CA   94619
(510) 569-5596 • fax: (510) 569-9161
e-mail: sstrong@projectchange.org
Web site: www.projectchange.org

Project Change began as an initiative aimed at reducing racial prejudice and improving race relations by helping implement a five-step process in local communities around the country. In 2002, Project Change entered into a partnership with the Claremont Graduate University Institute for Democratic Renewal to expand the scope of its mission in helping communities to combat racial injustice.

YWCA of the U.S.A.
1015 18th Street NW, Suite 1100, Washington, DC   20036
(202) 467-0801 • fax: (202) 467-0802
e-mail: info@ywca.org
Web site: www.ywca.org

The YWCA of the U.S.A. operates in more than 4,000 locations throughout the country in 400 associations in all 50 states. Its outreach extends internationally through its membership in the World YWCA. For decades, the YWCA has pioneered efforts to eliminate racism through programs and advocacy. The organization's vision of empowering women through the elimination of racism and sexism remains its driving force. The organization's Office of Racial Justice and Human Rights provides resources, training, and technical assistance to the local community and student YWCA associations to develop collaborative programs and strategies with other organizations to eliminate institutional racism at the local level in education, law enforcement, housing, health care, finance, and other institutions.

Bibliography

Books

Mark Aronson   *Race: A History Beyond Black and White*. New York: Simon and Schuster, 2007.

Earnest N. Bracey   *On Racism: Essays on Black Popular Culture, African American Politics, and the New Black Aesthetics*. New York: University Press of America, 2003.

Faye J. Crosby   *Affirmative Action Is Dead: Long Live Affirmative Action*. New Haven, CT: Yale University Press, 2004.

Joe R. Feagin   *Racist America: Roots, Current Realities, and Future Reparations*. New York: Routledge, 2001.

George M. Frederickson   *Racism: A Short History*. Princeton, NJ: Princeton University Press, 2002.

Charles A. Gallagher   *Rethinking the Color Line: Readings in Race and Ethnicity*. New York: McGraw-Hill, 2008.

Tariq Modood   *Multicultural Politics: Racism, Ethnicity, and Muslims in Britain*. Minneapolis: University of Minnesota Press, 2005.

Mark A. Noll   *God and Race in American Politics: A Short History*. Princeton, NJ: Princeton University Press, 2008.

Lucky Rosenbloom	*Liberal Racism Creates the Black Conservative: Issues and New Perspectives.* Lincoln, NE: iUniverse, 2006.
David O. Sears	*Racialized Politics: The Debate About Racism in America.* Chicago, IL: University of Chicago Press, 2000.
Derald Wing Sue	*Overcoming Our Racism: The Journey to Liberation.* San Francisco, CA: Jossey-Bass, 2003.
Abigail Thernstrom and Stephen Thernstrom	*Beyond the Color Line: New Perspectives on Race and Ethnicity in America.* Stanford, CA: Hoover Press, 2007.
Howard Winant	*The New Politics of Race: Globalism, Difference, Justice.* Minneapolis: University of Minnesota Press, 2004.

Periodicals

Tim Arango	"Before Obama, There Was Bill Cosby," *New York Times*, November 8, 2008.
Elizabeth Atkins	"Do Light-Skinned Black People Have an Advantage?" *Ebony*, February 2008.
K.C. Baker	"You Can't Live Here . . . (Unless You're White)," *Good Housekeeping*, April 2007.
Peter Baker	"Whose President Is He Anyway?" *New York Times*, November 16, 2008.

Haim Baram   "Israel's Secret Fears," *New Statesman*,
                    May 19, 2008.

Julio Cammarota   "Disappearing in the Houdini
                    Education: The Experience of Race
                    and Invisibility Among Latina/o
                    Students," *Multicultural Education*,
                    Fall 2006.

Benedict Carey   "Tolerance over Race Can Spread,
                    Studies Find," *New York Times*,
                    November 7, 2008.

Anne Chapman   "Race and Gender," *Black Enterprise*,
                    February 2008.

Yusuf Davis   "Where Are the African-American
                    Baseball Players?" Ebony, May 2007.

Sean Gardiner   "Runnin' Scared," *Village Voice*, April
                    30–May 6, 2008.

Nancy Gibbs   "This Is Our Time," *Time*, November
                    17, 2008.

David Glenn   "Our Hidden Prejudices, On Trial,"
                    Chronicle of Higher Education, April
                    25, 2008.

Sally Lehrman   "Omitting Race: Politically Correct or
                    Good Crime Reporting?" *The Quill*,
                    May 2008.

Tod Lewan   "Multiracial Americans See Attitudes
                    Evolving," *Ann Arbor News*, June 15,
                    2008.

Bonnie Mann   "Gay Marriage and the War on
                    Terror," *Hypatia*, Winter 2007.

Adam Nossiter   "For South, a Waning Hold on National Politics," *New York Times*, November 11, 2008.

Jennifer Olapido   "Global Warming Is Color-Blind," *Orion*, November–December 2007.

Ronald Roach   "Black Student Enrollment Rebounds at UCLA," *Diverse*, December 13, 2007.

Victor C. Romero   "Critical Race Theory in Three Acts: Racial Profiling, Affirmative Action, and the Diversity Visa Lottery," *Albany Law Review*, Winter 2002.

Lillian B. Rubin   "Fire and Flood: What a Difference Class and Race Makes, or Did Brian Williams See the News," *Dissent*, Winter 2008.

William H. Tucker   "The Ideology of Racism," *UN Chronicle*, September 2007.

George Yancey   "Experiencing Racism: Differences in the Experiences of Whites Married to Blacks and Non-Black Racial Minorities," *Journal of Comparative Family Studies*, Spring 2007.

Gary Younge   "Obama and the Power of Symbols," *Nation*, June 30, 2008.

Index